THE COSMOLOGY OF REINCARNATION AND REBIRTH

A brief history of reincarnation and rebirth and the evolution of past life regression therapy

by

CAROLE LOUIE

WWW.OAKLEAPRESS.COM

The Cosmology of Reincarnation and Rebirth: A brief history of reincarnation and rebirth and the evolution of past life regression therapy © 2024 by Carole Louie. All rights reserved. No part of this book may be used or reproduced in any manner whatsoever without written permission except in the case of brief quotations embodied in critical articles and reviews. For information visit:

www.OakleaPress.com

DEDICATION

With gratitude to Joel Whitton, Joe Fisher, Helen Waumbach, Dick Sutphen, William J. Baldwin, Roger Woolger, Michael Newton, Walter Semkiw, Dolores Cannon, and all who led the way before us.

TABLE OF CONTENTS

Foreword 6
INTRODUCTION 12
1 A BRIEF HISTORY OF REINCARNATION 15
   Prehistory
   Early Historical Records
   Nineteenth Century to Present
2 DISCOVERING MANY BELIEFS 51
   Transmigration/Reincarnation/Rebirth
   Karma/Dharma
   Jains
   Hinduism
   Buddhism
   Taoism
   Indigenous tribes
   African tribes
   Kabbalism
   Druze
   Theosophy
   Anthroposophy
   Channeled teachings about reincarnation
   A Scientific Approach
   Revelations from Regression Therapy

Table of Contents

3 THE EVOLUTION OF REGRESSION THERAPY .. 94
  Sleep Temples 2000 BCE–Early Hypnosis
  From Animal Magnetism/Mesmerism to Hypnosis
  From Hypnosis to Past Life Regression Therapy
4 MY COSMOLOGY 120
GLOSSARY 134
REFERENCE LIST 147
ABOUT THE AUTHOR 163
END NOTES 165

Foreword

Close your eyes and see inside of you; you will cross into new dimensions and witness the radiant shine of your soul. When you embrace introspection to discover your inner depths, you awaken your inner eyes by closing your physical eyes, revealing secret layers inside yourself. You transcend ordinary perception and enter regions of self-discovery, where the brilliance of your soul's essence illuminates your path to self-awareness and evolution.

The Cosmology of Reincarnation and Rebirth is a book that explores the fascinating world of life and death and the concept of reincarnation. This book, written by Carole Louie, offers readers a comprehensive overview of reincarnation and the evolution of past life regression therapy. It aims to provide readers with a cross-cultural introduction to reincarnation, organized chronologically from the earliest beliefs to present-day research. The author's firsthand experiences and research have led her to believe that the cosmology of reincarnation and rebirth expands our worldview beyond the physical and non-physical realms.

Life and death are two sides of the same coin. Death is a natural part of life, and it is something that we will all experience at some point. However, the concept of reincarnation offers us a new perspective on death. It teaches us that death is not the end but a transition to a new life. The value of reincarnation is that it offers a deeper understanding of life and death. It teaches us that death is not an end but a chance for a do-over. Reincarnation also offers us a deeper understanding of the purpose of our existence. It teaches us that we are not just citizens of one country or century but also time travelers with unrestricted passports. We are co-creators of our own destiny, and our actions in this life will impact our future lives.

Throughout history, humanity has been captivated by the profound questions surrounding the nature of the soul and its purpose in the grand tapestry of life. In this book, we embark on an extraordinary journey, guided by ancient wisdom, scientific discoveries, and personal narratives, to uncover the eternal truths that lie beyond the threshold of mortal existence. Intertwining the threads of spiritual traditions, philosophical musings, and scientific inquiry, *Cosmology* sheds light on the intricate dance between the soul and its mortal vessel. From the awe-inspiring process of birth to the mysterious passage of death, this book reveals the profound interplay between the physical and the metaphysical, the transient and the eternal.

The belief in reincarnation is a complex and diverse phenomenon that has left its mark on various cultures and philosophies. Pythagoras was an ancient Greek philosopher who remembered past lives and had insight into the transmigrations of his soul and others. Although he left no writings behind, his teachings influenced philosophers like Socrates, Plato, and Aristotle during the fifth and fourth centuries BCE.

The belief in reincarnation has traversed various philosophical and religious landscapes, imprinting how humans

The Cosmology of Reincarnation

perceive life, death, and the soul's journey. *Cosmology* goes beyond mere speculation, weaving together the latest scientific research and spiritual insights to understand the soul's voyage through time and space. Drawing from fields as diverse as quantum physics, psychology, and ancient mysticism, this book provides a multidimensional perspective that challenges conventional boundaries and expands our vision of what it means to be human. Reincarnation, the belief in the cycle of birth, death, and rebirth of the soul into different bodies, holds a significant place in the spiritual and religious beliefs of various cultures across history.

The Druze religion, predominantly found in regions like Lebanon, Syria, Jordan, and Israel, emphasizes the concept of reincarnation. The Druze hold that the number of souls remains constant throughout epochs, and their doctrine asserts that souls are continuously reborn in different bodies. The Druze differ from mainstream Muslims in many ways, including their scriptures, practices, and unique perspectives on reincarnation.

The Druze faith encompasses complex beliefs in which reincarnation plays a pivotal role. Their souls are thought to transfer only to bodies within their community, and a person must be born to Druze parents to be considered part of the faith. Reincarnation is central to their spiritual framework, although distinct from karma-driven concepts in other cultures. Notably, their views on reincarnation align with specific Neoplatonic ideas.

Whether through the Druze religion's intricate reincarnation doctrine, Sufism's openness to exploration, or its integration into the philosophical underpinnings of different eras, reincarnation remains an enduring and fascinating aspect of humanity's spiritual journey. Incorporating perspectives from various cultures, the concept of reincarnation continues to influence thought and belief systems.

Ian Stevenson, M.D. founded and directed the Division of Perceptual Studies at the University of Virginia School of Medicine. He was renowned for his scientific approach to his research into over twenty-five hundred cases of children who remembered past lives. He became interested in reincarnation because of a "growing feeling of dissatisfaction that available knowledge of heredity and environmental influences...often didn't account for personality as we see it."

In this book, the author will look at worldwide beliefs about the fascinating concept of reincarnation, where souls embark on a cyclical odyssey of rebirth, carrying with them the imprints of past lives and the potential for spiritual growth. The book delves into the tapestry of memories and karmic patterns, unveiling the transformative power of this timeless cycle and the lessons it imparts to our individual and collective evolution.

The exploration of channeled teachings about reincarnation offers insights into diverse spiritual perspectives. Channelers are individuals who communicate with entities from different planes of existence, sharing teachings on topics like reincarnation. These entities may range from evolved beings to groups with various levels of consciousness. The channeled teachings presented here delve into reincarnation, encouraging readers to consider the proposed ideas and discern their resonances with personal beliefs. As humanity continues to ponder the mysteries of the universe, channeled teachings pose thought-provoking questions, like the historical "Copernican moments" that have prompted paradigm shifts in understanding. This section explores the profound insights of several notable channelers, shedding light on the intricate tapestry of existence and the potential for growth through multiple lifetimes.

When examining reincarnation, personal growth, or the secrets of human awareness, the writer endeavors to introduce the usage of regression therapy. Past life regressions can be a captivating narrative tool for delving into characters' past lives, allowing readers to think about the interconnectivity of lives and the concept of karma. This strategy can offer depth to the story's spiritual or philosophical themes while piquing the reader's interest in the unexplained aspects of existence.

As the preface to this enthralling new book unfolds, it draws readers into a universe of profound reflection centered on the perplexing themes of reincarnation, death, and rebirth. The voyage across its pages promises to dig into the subtleties of existence beyond the present moment, with delicate strands of life's mysteries interlaced throughout. Curiosity and contemplation are fueled by the investigation of whether rebirth occurs instantly after death or if it transcends time's restrictions.

The Cosmology of Reincarnation

Cosmology explores the ethereal waltz between life, death, and the undiscovered places in between in a world through the cycles of reincarnation.

Khattar Hatoum, Ph.D.
President-American Druze Society, Virginia Chapter

INTRODUCTION

A book about the cosmology of reincarnation and rebirth is a resource I wish had been available when I began exploring reincarnation. As more people are accepting the concept of reincarnation but are bombarded by so much information, I was inspired to write this book to make reincarnation easier for others to understand. The first section of my book is a cross-cultural introduction to reincarnation organized chronologically from the earliest beliefs to present-day research. The second section describes the differences and similarities of reincarnation belief systems. To my surprise, regression therapy has a much longer history than I imagined. The third chapter covers the evolution of regression therapy as a powerful healing experience.

I leave it to the readers to choose which concepts resonate with them or which do not, or even to be selective about this banquet of ideas.

The Cosmology of Reincarnation and Rebirth offers a menu of reincarnation ideas and at the very least "food for thought" on your spiritual journey. Whether it is a snack, a feast, or a staple is up to you.

Observing the development of incarnations leads to a deeper understanding of our relationship with ourselves and the world, and our part as co-creators of it. When we use the scientific method to assess and validate theories

As the watch passes from hand to hand in room to room in the factory, one part being added here, and another there, until the delicate machine is perfected, according to the design conceived in the mind of the master before the work was begun; so, according to ancient philosophy, the first divine conception of man takes shape little by little, in the several departments of the universal workshop, and the perfect human being finally appears on our scene... This teaches that nature never leaves her work unfinished.

> Joseph Head and S. L. Cranston,
> *Reincarnation: The Phoenix Fire Mystery*

and modify old ideas as new evidence emerges, we must re-evaluate previous understandings of reincarnation against the latest body of information, and test/validate new theories for their efficacy in our current lives.

I sense a growing desire in the collective population to understand who one is within the cosmos. That desire might come from a need to know why terrible things happen. It might come from an increase in time to reflect on life. For many, religion does not answer these deep-seated questions and science creates more questions than answers. I hope that *The Cosmology of Reincarnation and Rebirth* adds more pieces to the puzzle.

For me, the cosmology of reincarnation and rebirth research expands my worldview beyond the physical and non-physical realms.

1 A BRIEF HISTORY OF REINCARNATION

Prehistory

Over 200,000 years ago, *Homo naledi* buried their deceased in the **Rising Star Cave** system near Johannesburg, in South Africa.[1] The Dinaledi Chamber, where 1,500 fossil specimens belonging to at least 15 individuals were found, lies at the end of several passageways that are extremely challenging for modern humans to reach. This begs us to think about what early man felt about his clansmen that caused him to carry the deceased body to such a hard-to-reach location. It was not an isolated incident as many other fossil excavations show.

Mtoto is Swahili for "child" and refers to a two-and-a-half to three-year-old child who was buried with extraordinary care. Mtoto's body was tucked in a fetal position, wrapped in a shroud with a pillow at its head, and buried in a gravesite some 78,000 years ago near Kenya, Africa.[2]

Another infant from **Border Cave** in South Africa was buried approximately 74,000 years ago with a pierced shell ornament covered in pigment.[3] Do these burial practices reveal an emotional bond between the dead children and those who laid them to rest? At the very least, these events raise the question of why humans started burying their dead in the first place.

The Cosmology of Reincarnation

Funeral rites and evidence of the capacity to show empathy for others among Neanderthal man 40,000 years ago were discovered in the **Shanidar Caves** in the Bradost Mountains of Northern Iraq.

These examples indicate cultural and moral development that life has meaning and are clues to the earliest forms of shamanic practices and ancestor worship. Human beings have gone through extensive physical evolution. Evidence of the development of tools, communication, working together to hunt, farm, and migrate as well as the development of cave art, pottery, ritual as in burial ceremonies, writing, recording, clothing, shelter, and trade show us an evolution of consciousness.

Recent studies of the evolution of religion indicate its beginnings in animism, the animation of all natural things including the belief in personal souls. A belief in animism progressed to a belief in an afterlife—a belief in survival of the individual personality beyond death.

Shamanism developed as a universal belief of Paleolithic hunter-gatherers that focused on communication with ancestral spirits as well as other spirits. Shamans became healers, ritual leaders, and mediators of the community. As humans migrated out of Africa more than 60,000 years ago, the shaman's skills enhanced survival. The studies show shamanism co-evolved with ancestral worship (contact with the spirits of the departed), the rudimentary beginning of the belief in the rebirth of one's ancestors and of religion.[4]

The Cosmology of Reincarnation

Many shamanic practices including ancestral worship are considered the earliest form of worship among all races. For hundreds of thousands of years, the history of a culture and its shamanic practices were passed from one generation to another by oral tradition until the evolution of written communication.

Early Historical Records

Banpo Village, a Neolithic site in the Yellow River Valley located east of Xi'an in Shaanxi Province, People's Republic of China, was occupied from c. 4500–3750 BCE. Stone tools and artifacts, tombs, six large kilns, storage pits, and almost one hundred foundations of buildings have been excavated at the site. Scratch marks on ceramic shards suggest the people in Banpo may have developed a system of writing long before the traditional date of the rise of literacy in China during the Shang Dynasty.

Writings on the **"oracle bones"** at Anyang, China of the Shang Dynasty (1600–1050 BCE) refer to earlier people, divination, relationships with ancestors, as well as sacrificial practices and the afterlife. Historian Harold M. Tanner said, "oracle bones are the earliest written records in Chinese civilization."[5] They were primary sources for the history of the Shang Dynasty thanks to the careful records of the diviners and are considered the earliest records of shamanic practices.

In India, the **Vedas**, whose Sanskrit name means "knowledge," "vision," or "wisdom," are the oldest scriptures of Hinduism, dating from 1500–1200 BCE. Like the

UPANISHAD

"As the body is augmented by food and water, so the individual self, augmented by its aspirations, sense contact, visual impressions, and delusion, assumes successive forms in accordance with its actions."

Svetasvatara *Upanishad,* 5.11
Sixth-fifth century BCE

The Cosmology of Reincarnation

oracle bones, tradition suggests that they originate from an older oral tradition revealed to the sages. Later Vedic texts—the Upanishads and the Gita—further developed the teachings of the Vedas. Joe Fisher, author of *The Case for Reincarnation*, said, "Although Hinduism, the oldest religion in the world, dates to the fourth millennium BCE reincarnation was not clearly enunciated in its teachings until the sixth century BCE. No one can vouch for the source of the doctrine, but it was handed down, not by the Brahmins, but by an older, red race who were kin to the ancient inhabitants of Egypt and Chaldea."[6]

Another group in India, the **Jains,** are considered one of the oldest religions in the world. They trace their origin back millions of years to their progenitor Tirthankaras (supreme preachers of Dharma, meaning law, duty, or fixed decree). Their oral tradition was written into scriptures and texts c. 600 CE. Like the other Dharmic religions characterized by the concept of Dharma (Hinduism, Sikhism and Buddhism), Jainism shares concepts and doctrines such as karma and rebirth, holds similar festivals, and has a monastic tradition. In Northern India, Jainism influenced the Buddha's beliefs.

In the **Old Kingdom of Egypt** (2700–2200 BCE), history was written in its architecture, particularly in the stone structures of the pyramids where instructions served a religious role enabling the transformation of the deceased. In the period from 2080–1640 BCE, "coffin texts" carried the tradition for those who could afford them, and from 1550–50 BCE the *Egyptian Book of the Afterlife* made

The Cosmology of Reincarnation

the instructions more readily available. *Akh*/the spark of God, *Ba*/the eternal soul, *Ka*/spirit (lower energy that is not eternal and needs to be activated), and *Khat*/the physical element of being are some of the words they used to describe the earthly and afterlife experiences. They reveal an intricate belief in the afterlife. Dr. Margaret Murray, a distinguished Egyptologist, states that their belief in reincarnation is clearly shown in the names: Amonemhat I's name means "He who repeats births," Sensusert I's name means "He whose births live," and Setekhy I means "Repeater of births."[7]

Instructions written on the walls eventually formed *The Book of Coming Forth by Day* or *Spells for Going Forth by Day* (aka *The Egyptian Book of the Dead*) (1991–1802 BCE), a collection of spells that enable the soul of the deceased to navigate the afterlife.

In *Oldest Books in the World*, Isaac Myer states that for the ancient people of Egypt, life on earth had an infinite duration and that before birth in this world, one had been born and died in many other worlds.

In South America, the **Maya** (900 BCE–900 CE) believed the soul is bound to the body at birth and at death the soul goes to the afterlife, Xibalba. Communication with ancestors gave advice to descendants and guided them to burial ritual offering practices. The *Popol Vuh (Book of Community)* codices of the K'iche Maya tells the story of reincarnation. For the **Inca** (1000 BCE–1825 CE), the spirit of the dead, camaquen, would follow a long dark road with the assistance of a black dog who was able to see in the dark. They did not use cremation because they believed it would destroy their vital force and prevent passage to the afterworld.

Although not much is known directly from the **Celtic** cultures—a band of Indo-European tribes that stretched from Spain to the Black Sea and from Scotland to Italy (700 BCE–500 CE), the first century BCE Greek historian Diodurus gives us a brief overview of their beliefs. His communication with the Druids, the order of priests and high-ranking learned Celts, sheds light on their concepts of metensomatosis, the passage of the immortal soul from one human body to another after a period in the Otherworld. The transmigration would repeat until completely freed from matter. Archaeological finds further indicate their beliefs about the afterlife in their burial customs. Some Celts preferred cremation to ensure freedom of the soul while others buried their deceased, often with burial goods and/or animals dear to the departed, and even their slaves. Some were known for their "cult of the head," a ritualistic beheading because the soul was thought to reside in the head. Was this practice related to ancestral connections or was it to ensure the enemy did not cause havoc for the living?

According to Greek historian Herodutus (c. 484–425 BCE), **Orpheus** obtained the belief in transmigration (the passage of a soul into another body after death) from Egypt. The same is said of Greek philosopher **Pherecydes** of Syros (sixth century BCE), the master of Pythagoras, to whom he taught the doctrine of metempsychosis and the immortality of the soul.

The Cosmology of Reincarnation

Greek philosopher and mathematician **Pythagoras** (c. 579–c. 490 BCE) was given the surname Mnesarchides (one who remembers his origins). "He was an important champion of what was called the doctrine of metempsychosis, understood as the soul's transmigration into successive bodies. He himself had been (a) Aethalides, a son of Mercury; (b) Euphorbus, son of Panthus, who perished at the hands of Menelaus in the Trojan war; (c) Hermotimus, a prophet of Clazomenae, a city of Ionia; (d) a humble fisherman, and finally (e) the philosopher of Samos."[8]

Pythagoras is said to remember a life as Aethalides who was given the gift of memory of his soul's transmigrations as well as knowing the souls of others. Pythagoras left no writings, but his teachings lived on in the works of fifth-fourth century BCE philosophers Socrates, Plato, and Aristotle.[9]

In the Myth of Er in *The Republic*, Plato (c. 470–399 BCE) described a thousand-year interval between lives, souls being judged by the gods before being reborn, and choosing to be human or non-human animals in their next life depending on their temperaments. He described souls who were judged and sent to Elysium (the home of the blessed after death in Greek and Roman mythology) or to Hades (the land of the dead in Greek mythology ruled by the Greek god of the underworld), and souls made to drink from Lethe, the River of Forgetfulness, to erase their memories before reincarnating. Even though Greeks were aware of Indian philosophy, they did not adopt the karma doctrine.[10]

The Cosmology of Reincarnation

Did Taoist philosopher **Chuang Tzu**/Chuang Chou/Zhuangzi/Zhang Zhou (fourth century BCE) portray the idea of transmigration in his famous poem? "Once Chuang Chou dreamt that he was a butterfly. He did not know that he had ever been anything but a butterfly and was content to hover from flower to flower. Suddenly he woke and found to his astonishment that he was Chuang Chou. But it was hard to be sure whether he really was Chou and had only dreamt that he was a butterfly or was he really a butterfly and was only dreaming that he was Chou. Between a man and a butterfly there is necessarily a barrier. The transition is called metempsychosis."[11]

In ancient China, the Tao was seen as an expression of relentless cycles where the universe swings back and forth between yin and yang. **Lao Tzu**/Laozi (c. 604 BCE), regarded as the father of Taoism, appeared around the same time as Buddha, Pythagoras, and Confucius. He is known for the *Tao te Ching/Dao de Jing*, which can be translated as *The Classic of the Way and its Power*, aka *The Book of the Tao and Its Virtue*. Lionel Giles (1875–1958), a British sinologist, writer, and philosopher, described it as a "well-defined rudimentary outline of a great system of transcendental and ethical philosophy."[12]

Taoist traditions relate that Lao Tzu practiced Tao in previous incarnations as Po-Chang in the time of Yao (2356–2255 BCE), as Kwang Chang Tze in the era of Hwang Ti, the Yellow Emperor (2711–2598 BCE), and in the time of Fu-Hsi (2800s BCE), Hwang Ti's predecessor.

Taoists, unlike Buddhists, do not seek to stop the cycles

PADMASAMBHAVA

"If you want to know your past life, look at your present condition. If you want to know your future life, look at your present actions.""

> Padmasambhava,
> eighth century CE

of reincarnation but to follow the path of Tao to become one with Tao.

Siddhartha Gautama was from a royal family in Northern India (fifth century BCE), and his tribe of origin, the Shakyas, had a non-Vedic religious practice. His path led him to an awakening. After years of studying with ascetics, he attained enlightenment which led to the Buddhist movement, a movement that spread throughout Asia and the world. He was known as the Buddha/the Awakened One or Shakyamuni Buddha (Sage of the Shakyas). He is said to have remembered many past lives, but Buddha's belief of anatta (Pali) or anatman (Sanskrit), meaning *"no soul"* as a principle not as an entity, distinguished his concept of transmigration from Hinduism. He gave his deeper teachings to the Arhats (people who are more advanced on the spiritual path) and limited teaching to the lay people. For four hundred years, the Buddha's teachings were transmitted orally to disciples. His teachings developed into two schools of thought: Mahayana and Theravada.

Beliefs in reincarnation in the **Levant** (a large area in the Eastern Mediterranean region of Western Asia) were not as dominant as in the East, but they are part of certain **Judean, Christian,** and **Islamic** sects. Like the Eastern traditions, Judean teachings trace their beginnings to thousands of years ago. The teachings that began with Abraham were passed orally until written first in the Tanakh/Hebrew Bible (eighth/seventh centuries BCE–second/first centuries BCE).

The Cosmology of Reincarnation

Were reincarnation beliefs in the Levant influenced by Hinduism, Buddhism, or the ancient Greek philosophers? The Levant's geographical position as the crossroads between the East and West makes this highly possible.

Philo Judaeus, an Alexandrian philosopher (c. 20 BCE–50 CE), coordinates Judaic teachings with Platonic philosophy in his book *De Somniis*. He said, "the air is full of souls; those who are nearest to earth descending to be tied to mortal bodies, return to other bodies." He also wrote in *De Giantes* that "The law of some is to enter mortal bodies and after certain prescribed periods to be again set free. But those possessed of diviner structure are absolved from all local bonds of earth."

The first century CE Jewish historian **Flavius Josephus** matter-of-factly speaks of reincarnation in *The Jewish War* where he describes the "souls of those whose hand have acted madly against themselves are received by the darkest place in Hades" in his account of addressing some Jewish soldiers who were about to commit suicide rather than be captured by the Romans. He defines the three schools of Jewish philosophy: the Pharisees, the Sadducees, and the Essenes, where he shows that the

Essenes taught the soul's preexistence—the foundation for all reincarnation beliefs.

Reincarnation is also basic to Kabbalistic thinking. **Kabbalah**, literally "reception, tradition" or "correspondence," is an esoteric method, discipline, and school of thought in Jewish mysticism (c. third century BCE). It is said to represent the hidden wisdom within the Hebrew

The Cosmology of Reincarnation

Bible and esoteric teachings from Moses who was educated in Egypt. In the *Book of the Revolutions of Souls* in the *Zohar, the Book of Splendor*, the Kabbalistic classic, it states, "All souls are subject to the trials of transmigration; and men do not know the designs of the Most High with regard to them...The souls must re-enter the absolute substance whence they have emerged. But to accomplish this end they must develop perfections, the germ of which is planted in them."

Another Jewish movement which began in the eighteenth-century CE among Jews in present-day Ukraine and other parts of Eastern Europe, **Hasidism** (or Chassidism) holds reincarnation as a universal belief. In the Hasidic play *The Dybbuk*, Solomon Judah Rapoport, who used the pen name S. Ansky, wrote, "No human life goes to waste...The souls of the dead do return to earth, but not as disembodied spirits. Some must pass through many forms before they achieve purification."

Unlike Christian orthodoxy, reincarnation was a universal teaching among the **Gnostics**, a parallel movement that claimed a close connection with the early Jesus movement, which had many names before "Christianity." One of those names was the Pre-existanta or Pre-existiani during the second century CE. Followers included Justin Martyr and Origen. Justin said that the soul inhabits a human body and a body of a wild beast more than once, but that it cannot remember previous experiences.[13] Origen, an early Christian scholar, taught universal salvation with the "restoration of all things" worked out across many lifetimes.[14]

"Like grass I have grown over and over again. I passed out of mineral form and lived as a plant. From plant I lifted up to be an animal. Then I put away the animal form and took on a human shape. Why should I fear that if I died, I shall be lost? For passing human form I shall attain the flowing locks and shining wings of angels. And then I shall become what no mind has ever conceived. O let me cease to exist! For non-existence only means that I shall return to Him."

    Jalaluddin Rumi (1207-1273 CE)

The Cosmology of Reincarnation

In 325 CE, the First Council of Nicaea convened by Roman Emperor Constantine ruled against reincarnation, and at the Second Council of Constantinople in 553 CE, Origen was declared heretical which led to suppression of beliefs and violence toward heretics.

In the period known as the **Dark Ages** (fifth-fourteenth century CE), Gnostic teachings continued. Its European bearers were known as Cathars and Albigenses. **Catharism** was the religion of catharsis, or purification. Edmond Holmes says that in their teaching, Jesus came, not to die for them, but to help them to save themselves by unfolding to them their origin and their destiny, and how best to accomplish their work through purifying cycles of metempsychosis.[15]

Why then was belief in reincarnation anathema to the Christian orthodoxy, to the correct or accepted creeds? We may never know, but we do know that this conflict led to the Inquisition, an institution within the Catholic Church which conducted trials to combat heresy. For several centuries, heretic-hunting raged its unparalleled fury, and hundreds of thousands paid the price. In the West, this was the dark ages for the teachings of reincarnation.

While **Islam** does not hold beliefs about reincarnation and the Quran makes no direct reference to it, some of its passages can be interpreted as referring to reincarnation. For instance, in Chapter 25/Surah Zakhraf/Mecca verses 5/10/6, it says, "And He sent down rain from above in proper quantity and He brings back to life the earth, similarly you shall be reborn." Was this the reason some Isma'ili's say that

The Cosmology of Reincarnation

Krishna reincarnated as Buddha and then Muhammad and does it explain the esoteric teachings of three aspects of rebirth: the periodical incarnation of the Perfect Man or Deity; the return of the Iman or other spiritual leader after death; and the return of all the ordinary souls?[16]

Sufism—the mystical branch of Islam—emerged early on in Islamic history partly as a reaction against the worldliness of the early Umayyad Caliphate (seventh century CE). Sufis believe that humankind has always been one with God and the path merely serves as remembrance of this realization, according to Grand Sheikh Idries Shah.[17]

Even though Islam's orthodoxy does not recognize reincarnation, Sufism leaves it up to its members to choose. Renowned thirteenth century CE Sufi poet Jalāl al-Dīn Rūmī (Jalaluddin Rumi) passionately believed in rebirth.[18]

Druze religion emerged in Egypt in 1017 CE as an off-shoot or subset of Islam and can be found in Lebanon, Syria, Jordan, Israel, and as immigrants in other countries. Druze is an exonym derived from the name of an Ismaili missionary known as ad-Darzī. They describe themselves as *al-muwahhidūn*, those who believe in the unity of God. The Druze doctrine of reincarnation/the transmigration of souls (*arwāh* [plural] *rūh* [singular]) states that the number of souls has remained constant in every epoch. A previous life is called *jīl mādā*, "past generation," and *amalīyatan-nu☐q* refers to one's previous life families.

Druze differ from mainstream Muslims in many important respects such as their scriptures and by not ob-

The Cosmology of Reincarnation

serving the five fundamental tenets of Islam. Druze religious scriptures are kept secret from non-Druze and from the *juhhal* (about 90% of the community) who are not initiated into their religion, while the *uqqal* go through religious training and are initiated into their religion. The Druze became a closed system. A person is considered Druze only if born to parents who are both Druze and is obligated to marry within the group. Reincarnation is a foremost principle. Druze are influenced by Neoplatonic philosophy; however, their reincarnation beliefs state that a human soul will transfer only to a human body; that a male Druze can be reincarnated only as another male Druze and a female Druze only as another female Druze, and they cannot be reincarnated in the body of a non-Druze. Even though James Matlock said that for the Druze, reincarnation is not associated with karma, this mantra from the Druze sacred text *The Epistles of Wisdom* or *Rasa'il al-Hikmah* suggests the law of cause and effect:

ان الله غني عن عبادتكم منزه عن ديانتكم لا ينقص من ملكه شيا ولا يزيد من ملكه شيا

و انما هي اعمالكم التي ترد ا ليكم

"God does not need your worship, or your religious beliefs, nor does it increase His power in the slightest. Rather, it is your deeds that are returned to you."

The Dark Ages (fifth-fourteenth century CE) and the Inquisition (twelfth-seventeenth century CE) slowed the spread of the study of reincarnation in the West. The Dark Ages were followed by the **Renaissance period** (1300-1700 CE) and by a time of scientific and technological ad-

"There is no doubt that through our actions, we are trying to achieve perfection and to remove imperfections. If our world is based on a just and moral order, then it is imperative that we should one day achieve this goal. But most people whom we know are not able to achieve this goal in one life. Therefore, it is only logical for us to believe that there must be a life after this life, so that we can achieve this goal. Otherwise, we have to give up our faith in justice, order, and perfection."

>Immanuel Kant
>(German philosopher, 1724-1804)

vancements: the Humanist Movement (fourteenth-fifteenth centuries CE) and the Reformation Movement (sixteenth century CE). Scientific exploration by people such as Galileo di Vincenzo Bonaiuti de' Galilei and Leonardo da Vinci planted seeds for a new worldview untethered by religious dogma. Martin Luther's challenge of Catholic doctrine led the way for spiritual reformation. Francesco Petrarca (commonly anglicized as Petrarch) inspired **Humanism**, the intellectual movement, with his discoveries of lost ancient manuscripts. The invention of the printing press made information more accessible to the masses and played a part in the next phase of human evolution. By the seventeenth century CE, ideas of reincarnation in England and Europe were circulated among esoteric exponents.

In 1612, **William Strachey**, an Englishman, wrote *The Historie of Travaile into Virginia Britannia* based on his time as Secretary to the colony in 1610-1611 CE. His conversations with literate Powhatans gave him a unique view of the life and beliefs of the Indigenous people, including their belief in reincarnation. As a scholar versed in Pythagoras' concepts of reincarnation, Strachey compared the Powhatan's beliefs to those of the ancients.[19]

Two Hundred Queries Moderately Propounded Concerning the Doctrine of the Revolution of Humane Souls, and Its Conformity to the Truths of Christianity by a Christian Kabbalist, **Franciscus Mercurius van Helmont**, was the first book in English on reincarnation (1684). In it, he constructed the theory of soul evolution (reincarnation), limited to twelve incarnations spanning a period of one thousand years directed toward the perfection of the soul. George Keith was instrumental in publishing the book and eventually brought reincarnation theory to America in the 1690s, where he promoted it among the American Quakers. However, the controversy about reincarnation split the Philadelphia Quakers into two groups.

The Dark Ages were followed by **The Age of Reason** (eighteenth century CE), an age precipitated by Isaac Newton's discovery of a fundamental universal order and the **Enlightenment** philosophers who advocated a logical and scientific approach to religious and social matters.

The Age of Reason had a profound effect on **America's Founding Fathers** (1700s). Several of the signers of the Declaration of Independence and Constitution were Freemasons and were familiar with the Greek classics including Plato's *Republic*. Freemasonry does not require any specific belief in the afterlife, only that the soul is immortal—that some aspect of who we are continues in some way after physical death. Those who believe in reincarnation, like those who believe in immediate heavenly reward, do not live for the moment, except as a prelude to a future. What we do now has real ramifications for our future in this life and the next (and the next).

Freemasons can have a broad perspective on reincarnation. "What better way to be humbled than to realize that our spiritual work is bigger than our single lifetime? Masonry, like the Operative Craft of cathedral builders, teaches us that we must start what others will finish and finish what others have begun, spanning lifetimes and generations. We cannot expect to accomplish everything in our short lives, and we shouldn't bemoan it as a personal failing. What a strange thing it would be in God's grand plan for us to only live and die, when there are more important things that need time to move toward eternity, no matter how the rest of our journeys turn out."[20]

One of those Founding Fathers was **Benjamin Franklin** whose epitaph, written when he was twenty-two years old, speaks volumes about his understanding:

The body of B. Franklin, Printer, like the cover of an old book, its contents torn out and stripped of its lettering and gilding, lies here food for worms, but the work shall not be lost, for it will as he believed appear once more in a new and more elegant edition revised and corrected by the author.[21]

Although it was not used on his tombstone, he wrote in his seventy-ninth year: "When I see nothing annihilated and not a drop of water wasted, I cannot suspect the annihilation of souls, or believe that God will suffer the daily waste of millions of minds readymade that now exist and put Himself in the continual trouble of making new ones. Thus, finding myself to exist in the world, I believe I shall, in some shape or other, always exist; and, with all the inconveniences human life is liable to, I shall not object to a new edition of mine, hoping, however, that the *errata* of the last may be corrected."[22]

The Cosmology of Reincarnation
Nineteenth Century to Present

By the 1800s, **American Esotericism** and **Transcendentalism** emerged, and the ideas of reincarnation evolved from the ancient Greek and Hindu teachings to influence Walt Whitman, Henry Thoreau, Bronson Alcott, Ralph Waldo Emerson, and others. Emerson said that "the complete human requires multiple lives that will allow the soul to drink the healing waters of illumined thought" and that all of nature evolves toward its higher potential.

At the same time, another influence developed with the importation of African people as slaves. Their beliefs centered around the role of ancestral souls and ceremonies to remember them. Folk tales by African Americans showed clear beliefs in reincarnation, including transmigration.[23]

In late 1875, the **Theosophical Society** was founded in New York City by Helena Petrovna Blavatsky, Colonel Henry Steel Olcott, William Quan Judge, and others who were in search of Ancient Wisdom. Mme. Blavatsky was a Russian woman who traveled all over the world in search of wisdom about life and the reason for human existence. She brought the spiritual wisdom of the East and that of the ancient Western mystery schools to the modern West, an innovative idea in the Victorian age.

The Theosophical movement became worldwide with centers in North America, Europe, and India. Even though "acceptance of reincarnation was not a requirement for membership allowing freedom of thought being the cardinal principle of theosophical education," Mme.

The Cosmology of Reincarnation

Blavatsky said, "Karma and reincarnation are in reality the A, B, C of theosophy."[24] She published *Isis Unveiled* (1877) about her Theosophical worldview, followed by *The Secret Doctrine* (1888), a commentary on what she claimed were ancient Tibetan manuscripts.[25]

Blavatsky merges Indic with Gnostic and Kabbalistic sources embracing karma and reincarnation as a "cycle of necessity" where a "Monad" was reborn only as a human or higher being once it attained human status. Monad (Ancient Greek) refers to a basic or original substance. The human being traveled a long journey until he/she returned to Source. Blavatsky said the time between incarnations lasted from one to three thousand years, and that Theosophy associates karma and reincarnation with the process of evolution of consciousness into self-realization. Ian Stevenson and James Matlock refer to Theosophical karmic beliefs as "retributive karma," aka "juridical karma," where there are direct consequences to actions.

Two people who were part of the Theosophical Society movement are worth noting for their contributions to the evolution of the concepts about reincarnation: Rudolf Steiner (1861-1925), Austrian occultist, social reformer, architect, esotericist, clairvoyant, speaker, and writer, and Jiddu Krishnamurti (1895-1986), a philosopher, mystic, speaker and writer.

Rudolf Steiner was a regular speaker at the Theosophical Society. He sought a Western approach to spirituality based on the philosophical and mystical traditions of European culture—a synthesis of science and spirituality which he called "spiritual science." Although not officially a member, he became the head of the German section of the Theosophical Society in 1902 and leader of the Theosophical Esoteric Society for Germany and Austria in 1904. Steiner added his perspective to the Theosophical teachings.

In 1912–13, after a disagreement about the claim that Krishnamurti was destined to be the new Maitreya, Steiner and members of the German section of the Theosophical Society broke off to form a new group, the **Anthroposophical Society**.

He was a prolific speaker and writer. His series of lectures about reincarnation were compiled in *Reincarnation and Karma* where he describes the development of feeling memory and how karmic effects pass between incarnations.

Steiner was not without controversy on several issues, such as his beliefs about Jesus, his support of the attitude that Jews should assimilate into society, and by criticism that considered some anthroposophical practices pseudoscience. Although the Anthroposophical Society and other esoteric movements were banned by the Nazi government, there were staunch supporters within prominent members of the Nazi party. Some Anthroposophical members were pro-Nazi, but others were not.

Jiddu Krishnamurti was born in Southern India. In 1909, he was recognized by Theosophist Charles Leadbeater as the "vehicle for the Lord Maitreya," who would be an advanced spiritual entity to guide the evolution of humankind according to Theosophical doctrine. To that end, Krishnamurti and his brother Nityananda (Nitya) were taken into the Theosophical Society in India under the tutelage of Annie Besant. The Order of the Star in the East (OSE) was formed in 1911 and Krishnamurti was named head of the order as he was cultivated by the Theosophists; however, in 1922, he had a life-changing experience, a mystical awakening. He eventually left the Theosophical Society, spent years processing his mystical experience, and established the Krishnamurti Foundation. Before his death in 1986, he declared that nobody should succeed him, but that people must find their own way. He compared himself with Thomas Edison, but now it was up to others to "flick the switch."

D.T. Suzuki/Daisetsu Teitaro Suzuki (1870-1966) was a Japanese American Buddhist monk, essayist, philosopher, religious scholar, translator, and writer. Instrumental in the spread of Zen Buddhism as a practical religion, Suzuki was also influenced by Western esotericism and Theosophy. He said, "We can conceive of the soul as not entering a body...creating a body suitable for its habitation...the soul comes first, and the body is constructed by it. This is really the Buddhist conception of transmigration...We think of the soul not as an entity, but as a principle."[26] He summed the Buddha's teachings up as follows, "Enlightenment is seeing the absolute ego reflected in the relative ego and acting through it."[27]

Known as the "Sleeping Prophet" and a devout Christian healer and clairvoyant who went into a trance to gain

The Cosmology of Reincarnation

information for his clients, **Edgar Cayce** (1877-1945) was startled when a "reading" for Arthur Lammers in 1923 revealed a past life answer to his queries. Lammers asked questions about the mechanics of the subconscious, the difference between spirit and soul as well as the reasons for personality and talent. He wanted to know what Cayce would say while in a trance about the Kabbala, the mystery schools of Egypt, the mystics of Tibet, even Madame Blavatsky and Theosophy. He asked Cayce questions that no one had presented to him: "What is the real nature of the soul and what is the purpose of this experience on earth?...What were we doing before we came here?"[28] Under trance, to his amazement Cayce answered that Lammer was a monk in a previous life.

Cayce overcame his doubt about being taken over by the devil and gradually accepted reincarnation. In fact, he saw Jesus as an adept who had materialized in twenty-nine previous incarnations. Cayce's readings would refer to a past life where applicable, and he predicted his next incarnation.[29] He created the Association for Research and Enlightenment in Virginia Beach, Virginia as a healing and educational center.

Another well-known and beloved Indian spiritual teacher who came to the West was **Paramahansa Yogananda** (1870-1952). Born Mukunda Lal Ghosh, he was a disciple of the Bengali yoga guru Swami Sri Yukteswar Giri who sent him to spread the teachings of yoga to the West. His mission was to embrace the unity between Eastern and Western religions and a balance between Western material growth and Indian spirituality through meditation and Kriya Yoga.

He remembered several past lives, including a life in England. Did the memory of that life help him bridge the divide between the East and West? He described reincarnation as a change of "mortal dress:"

How many times you have changed your clothing in this life, yet because of this you would not say that you have changed. Similarly, when you give up this bodily dress at death you do not change. You were just the same, and immortal soul, a child of God. Reincarnation means the change of mortal dress. But your real self will never change. You must concentrate on your real self, not on your body, which is nothing but a garment.[30]

Focusing on meditation, Kriya Yoga, and self-realization as the knowing in body, mind, and soul that we are one with the omnipresence of God, Yogananda established the Yogoda Satsanga Society of India in 1917 and the Self-Realization Fellowship (SRF) in California in 1920. His life story, *Autobiography of a Yogi*, was published in 1946 and is widely regarded as a modern spiritual classic.

Early memories of past life memories were recorded long before Ian Stevenson began his ground-breaking research. James Matlock and Erlendur Haraldsson document early accounts in *I Saw the Light and Came Here: Children's Experiences of Reincarnation* (2017) and in *Signs of Reincarnation: Exploring Beliefs, Cases, and Theory* by James Matlock (2019):

A first millennium case in China recorded by J.J.M. De Groot in 1901 of the reincarnation of Chang Khoh-khin.

The Cosmology of Reincarnation

A seventeenth century case in India of Ramdas who remembered his previous life as Rawat Subharam who died in 1699.

A nineteenth century case of a Syrian Druze boy who recalled his life as a man in Damascus.

John Wortabet, *Researches into the Religions of Syria* (1860): the case of twin Burmese boys who remembered their lives as Maung San Nyein and Ma Gwin who died in 1866.

In Harold Fielding Hall's *The Soul of a People* (1898), the case of Katsugoro who was born in 1815 and spoke of his life as Tozo which was recorded by Lafcadio Hearn (1898).

The details of these accounts are like Ian Stevenson's research.

Ian Stevenson (1918–2007) was a Canadian-born American psychiatrist and the founder and director of the Division of Perceptual Studies at the University of Virginia School of Medicine. He was renowned for his scientific approach to his research into over twenty-five hundred cases of children who remembered past lives. He became interested in reincarnation because of a "growing feeling of dissatisfaction that available knowledge of heredity and environmental influences...often didn't account for personality as we see it." This inspired him to explore the idea that emotions, memories, and even physical bodily features can be passed on from one incarnation to another. He traveled worldwide to conduct on-the-spot careful investigations of reported accounts of past life memories. Following strict protocols, he created a rigorous

The Cosmology of Reincarnation

criterion to determine where an account could be solved. Some of the unsolved cases showed good evidence, but he classified stronger accounts as "solved cases," weeding out anecdotal accounts no matter how fascinating.

Stevenson wrote fourteen books on reincarnation, including *Twenty Cases Suggestive of Reincarnation*, *Cases of the Reincarnation Type* (four volumes) (1966), and *Reincarnation and Biology: A Contribution to the Etiology of Birthmarks and Birth Defects* (1997). His over forty years of research set the stage for a different approach to the concept of reincarnation. Stevenson went as far as to say that "a rational man can, if he wants now, believe in reincarnation on the basis of evidence rather than simply on the basis of religious doctrine or cultural tradition."[31]

Born Nguy☐n Xuân B☐o in 1926 in Vietnam, **Thich Nhat Hanh**/Th☐y ("master; teacher") knew at an early age he wanted to become a monk. He received training in Vietnamese traditions of Mahayana and Theravada Buddhism; however, after disagreements with the older organizations, he evolved what he learned about Buddhism into a practice of "engaged Buddhism" and "mindfulness." At the same time, he became adept in several languages, in comparative religious studies, and science.

Like the Dalai Lama, Thich Nhat Hahn was forced to flee his homeland Vietnam in 1966. Likewise, his Buddhist teachings have had an impact worldwide. He eventually settled in Southern France where he created Plum Village Monastery and continued to advocate for an evolution of Buddhist beliefs through "mindfulness," non-violence, and

When asked what determines the time between incarnations, Seth replied, "You. If you are tired, then you rest. If you are wise, you take time to digest your knowledge and plan your next life, even as a writer plans his next book. If you have too many ties with this reality or if you are too impatient, or if you have not learned sufficiently, then you may return too quickly. It is always up to the individual. There is no predestination. The answers are within yourself then, as the answers are within you now."

The Case for Reincarnation by Joe Fisher

The Cosmology of Reincarnation

through his art and poems like *Please Call Me by My True Names*. The last stanza of the poem speaks to all who are awakening; "Please call me by my true names, so I can wake up, and so the door of my heart can be left open, the door of compassion."[32]

Unlike the Dalai Lama who has not returned to his homeland, Thich Nhat Hahn returned to Vietnam where he passed in 2022.

One of the preeminent figures in the world of paranormal phenomena, an example of a non-religious approach to reincarnation theory, **Jane Roberts** (1929–1984) was an American author, poet, psychic, and spirit medium. She channeled a being called Seth, whom Roberts described as an "energy personality essence no longer focused in physical matter." It began in 1963, when Roberts had an experience where she found herself "Between one normal minute and the next, a fantastic avalanche of radical, new ideas burst into my head with tremendous force... It was as if the physical world were really tissue-paper-thin, hiding infinite dimensions of reality, and I was flung through the tissue paper with a huge ripping sound." When she "came to," Roberts found herself writing notes with the title: *The Physical Universe as Idea Construction*.[33]

Like Edgar Cayce, Roberts went into a trance to channel the information she received from Seth, and like Cayce she initially had doubts about the messages. Roberts channeled messages from Seth for twenty-one years and published them in the *Seth Material* (1970). Roberts summarized the Seth material about reincarnation in *Ad-*

ventures in Consciousness (1975) from a psychological perspective, where the "focus personality" is the current identity, and the "source-self" is the core or transphysical identity. Each person has aspects which manifest through incarnate lifetimes. The present "now" is the current life. Through psychic contact with source-self, one can perceive other lives, which exist concurrently, and mutually influence both the past and the future. Every human being is a multidimensional being.[34]

Lhamo Dhondup was born in 1935, the year of the demise of the 13th Dalai Lama. When he was about two years old, a search party discovered and evaluated him by Tibetan Buddhist customs, and declared that he was the reincarnated **14th Dali Lama**. Like Krishnamurti, he was tutored as a spiritual leader, but unlike Krishnamurti, he became the 14th Dalai Lama. His spiritual name is Jetsun Jamphel Ngawang Lobsang Yeshe Tenzin Gyatso, known as Tenzin Gyatso. He is the current Dalai Lama, the highest spiritual leader and former head of state of Tibet. Although his exile from Tibet in 1959 due to the Chinese takeover was a loss for the Tibetan people, it was instrumental in bringing the Tibetan Buddhist teachings to the Western world and in creating interfaith dialogue worldwide. In an interview in 2014 the Dalai Lama stated, "the institution of the Dalai Lama has served its purpose." The question remains whether tradition will prevail, whether the Chinese government will have a say about the next reincarnation of this spiritual leader, or if indeed, there is no need for another Dalai Lama. For now, the 14th Dalai

Lama continues to touch the hearts and minds of Buddhists and non-Buddhists around the world with lessons on non-violence and compassion.

Reincarnation researcher **James G. Matlock**, Ph.D. (1954–) compiled years of in-depth investigations at the American Society of Psychical Research, the Rhine Research Center, and the Parapsychology Foundation into a course on reincarnation research. The course became a twelve-part series with Jeffrey Mishlove, Ph.D. on the New Thinking Allowed YouTube channel, and the book *Signs of Reincarnation: Exploring Beliefs, Cases, and Theory* (2019). His work inspired the Signs of Reincarnation Facebook page with over seventy-one thousand members and moved reincarnation research into the twenty-first century way of thinking and discussing the subject. He co authored *I Saw the Light and Came Here: Children's Experiences of Reincarnation* with Erlendur Haraldsson (2016).

In his seminal book *Lifecycles: Reincarnation and the Web of Life* (1990), **Christopher M. Bache**, Ph.D. said, "Adopting a reincarnationist world view can so change our perception of what we are and what we are involved in that it becomes impossible to continue playing the game by the old rules." *Lifecyles* is a combination of a scientific and philosophical approach to describe the dynamics of rebirth and of consciousness. And his book *LSD and the Mind of the Universe: Diamonds from Heaven* (2019) makes the case for psychedelic exploration of spiritual experience and pushes the boundaries beyond the cycles of reincarnation into Divine Oneness.

"Reincarnation gives us reason to ask larger questions about what we are and what our place in the scheme of things is. It also gives us cause to expect larger answers of these questions. When we begin to glimpse our true longevity, when we begin to appreciate the true scope of our lives, we can no longer see ourselves as simply the citizens of one country or one century. We must instead come to see ourselves as time travelers with unrestricted passports."

Christopher M. Bache, Ph.D.,
Lifecycles: Reincarnation and the Web of Life

Coming full circle, **Indigenous people** around the world continued their shamanic practices handed down from generation to generation in song, dance, art, and story as well as the belief in transmigration as a way of life. **Antonia Mills** and **Richard Slobodin's** book *Amerindian Rebirth: Reincarnation Belief Among North American Indians and Inuit* (1994) focuses on North America's Indian tribes but also a few other Indigenous people around the world. Most of these people have continued the belief in reincarnation for thousands of years even as colonization attempted to destroy their cultures and the world changed rapidly in modern times.

Their reincarnation beliefs affected every aspect of their lives, their relationship with the earth, with each other, and how they raise their children and care for their elders. They pay attention to announcing dreams and visions. They pay attention to signs that an ancestor has reincarnated, and they mark a deceased body with the hope of the mark appearing on a newborn. They understand the continuity of life, the connection of all relationships, one's purpose, and the importance of living in harmony with the Great Spirit and Universe.

Mircea Eliade, author of *Shamanism: Archaic Techniques of Ecstasy* (1951), believes that reincarnation concepts are part of an animistic (belief in spiritual beings concerned with human affairs) tradition that precedes shamanic techniques of ecstasy.

Ian Stevenson, reincarnation researcher and former head of the Department of Perceptual Studies at the University of Virginia, suggests that Tlingit (Indigenous peoples of the Pacific Northwest Coast of North American) beliefs may have come from the migration of Siberian reincarnation beliefs. DNA haplogroups evidence supports this migration hypothesis.

Referring to Hindus, Buddhists, and Amerindians, Antonia Mills added that "all three groups expect people to be reborn, bringing back traits they manifested in previous lives or occasionally manifesting traits desired to embody in a subsequent life." Richard Slobodin added, "One of the striking distinctions between reincarnation beliefs among tribal peoples of North America and the well-known rebirth concepts of South Asia is that to Native North Americans, reincarnations are an expansion of continuity, of survival, and of connectedness."

2 DISCOVERING MANY BELIEFS

Reincarnation beliefs evolved out of animism, shamanic practices, and ancestral worship. They are as varied as the cultures who embraced them.

In this section, we will look at reincarnation beliefs around the world. While there are similarities, there are noteworthy differences, starting with words. The evolution of words and transliteration of words from one language to another can be problematic. The aim here is to "keep it simple."

Transmigration/Reincarnation/Rebirth

Let us begin with the word ***transmigration***. "Trans" means beyond, and "migration" means change of residence. *Websters* defines transmigration as the migration of the soul to a different body after death, or to go from one state of existence or place to another.

There are two types of transmigration: metempsychosis and metensomatosis. **Metempsychosis** refers to the transmigration at death of the soul of a human being or animal into a new body of the same or a distinct species. **Metensomatosis**, on the other hand, refers to the passage of the immortal soul from one human body to another after a period in the Otherworld.

Reincarnation is currently used to describe all types of transmigration. It comes from Latin meaning "to be

The Cosmology of Reincarnation

made flesh again" and refers to a belief that a part of a being survives physical death to be reborn in a new body. For Hindus, reincarnation is the re-embodiment of a soul (atman) in a different body; however, for Buddhists, instead of a soul, a stream of consciousness (anatta, meaning "no soul") migrates from one body to another. For Hindus, soul (atman) is a spiritual or immaterial part of a human being or animal, but for Buddhists, there is no fixed essence or soul but a stream of consciousness that carries potential memories, volitions, and mental habits to another life. Buddhists refer to this process as **rebirth** and believe consciousness can be accessed through meditation, a near-death experience, or as a natural gift.

Even within Buddhist traditions there is much debate about anatta. As previously mentioned, the transliteration of words from one language to another can be problematic. The sixth century Chinese Tathāgatagarbha translation sums it up by describing anatta as *"beyond being."*

The ancient Greek classics used metempsychosis and transmigration to describe this process. Descriptions of the reincarnation beliefs of the Jain, Egyptian, Taoist, and Indigenous people are similar.

Greek historians described the Celtic belief as metensomatosis, which also is the case with Kabbalists, Hasidic Jews, and Cathars as well as with Edgar Cayce and others. Druze also adhere to a rebirth in a human form; however, it occurs without an intermission in the Otherworld. And yet others such as Sufis and mystics let individuals explore their beliefs on their own. Most faiths believe that after the life force leaves the body, it moves on to another existence, but not all agree about an immortal aspect of one's being.

In his book *Signs of Reincarnation: Exploring Beliefs, Cases, and Theory*, James Matlock describes **three types of reincarnation**: concurrent, replacement, and multiple simultaneous/soul splitting. Concurrent reincarnation is the belief that more than one spirit may occupy a single body simultaneously, while replacement reincarnation is the belief that a spirit replaces the original spirit without the body dying. It is referred to as *parakaja pravesh* (Sanskrit/Hindi), a possession by a wandering spirit. Multiple simultaneous reincarnation means a spirit occupies more than one body at the same time. It is also called soul splitting or split souls in New Age metaphysics. Matlock defines the spirit as a disembodied soul, mind, psyche, or stream of consciousness, and may be human or nonhuman. He defines the soul as the life force.

What exactly animates a body and consciousness? And what becomes of that aspect when the physical body dies? This is a question that has haunted many from the beginning and is now being explored by scientists, particularly after studies of near-death experiences (NDE). Just as archaeological and DNA research have given us a clearer picture about the evolution of humans, will science add to what the sages and shamans taught us about reincarnation/rebirth?

Today, transmigration, reincarnation, and rebirth are used interchangeably, but it is helpful to understand the differences.

Karma/Dharma

Karma is the principle of cause and effect where one's intentions and actions influence the future of one's life as well as the nature of future existences. Just as each tradition has nuances for transmigration, reincarnation, and rebirth, the meaning of karma differs between the various traditions.

Reincarnation researcher James Matlock identified **four categories of karma**: juridical, retributive, dispositional, and processional.

1. Juridical karma is the traditional view that the way we conduct ourselves in one life affects us in that life or another one.
2. Retributive karma is when direct justice manifests physically, such as an eye for an eye.
3. Dispositional karma, on the other hand, is an internal psychological law manifested in thoughts, feelings, and behavior. In Hinduism, dispositional karmic traits are called "samskaras."
4. Processional karma (coined by Matlock) operates within an individual's mind or psyche. It may involve self-judgment, but it originates from an internal force rather than an external one. This psychological force carries karma forward to an individual's personality and personal conflicts from life to life on a continuous stream of consciousness.

The Cosmology of Reincarnation

According to Matlock, the subconscious preserves the memory, behavioral dispositions, and personality, but memory is latent until it is drawn forth.

Dharma is the eternal and inherent nature of reality, an aspect of truth or reality. In Hinduism, it is a cosmic law underlying right behavior and social order. The purpose of dharma is to be in harmony with the supreme reality. For Jains, dharma is one's true nature. In Buddhism, it is the nature of reality regarded as a universal truth taught by the Buddha.

Next, we will look at reincarnation/rebirth beliefs by religions, cultures, or organizations.

Jains

As we begin to look at the reincarnation/rebirth beliefs in cultures around the world, we will start with the **Jains** who believe the path of reincarnation is a process of transmigration based on one's karma. It is not doled out by a deity but exists on its own as an innate moral order in the cosmos. It is self-regulating through the workings of the natural universal law of karma.

For Jains, karma is not a supernatural concept, but a physical object made of subtle particles of matter. Whenever you do an action, your karmic energy attaches to your soul/*jiva*. The soul carries these karmic particles around from one life to the next until a person removes them. For Jains, karma is divided into eight types. Each type has four subsets and each type of karma and its subset affects the soul in diverse ways. Jains believe actions that are harmful

You cannot see the seer of seeing;
You cannot hear the hearer of hearing;
You cannot think of the thinker of thinking;
You cannot know the knower of knowing.
This is yourself that is within all.
Everything else but this is perishable.

Bribadaranyaka *Upanishad*

or selfish add more karma than good deeds and that bad karma attracts other bad karma, so a person who commits bad acts will commit more. Jains seek liberation by clearing all karma, thus freeing themselves from the cycle of rebirth. They do so by following Jainism vows and living the Three Jewels/*Ratnatraya*: right vision, right knowledge, and right conduct.

Following Jain vows is living one's dharma. Non-violence/*Ahimsa* is the greatest dharma. Jainism distinguishes practices for a "layperson" versus an "ascetic," and teaches the ten virtues/*das-dharma*: forgiveness, humility, straightforwardness, truthfulness, purity, self-restraint, penance, renunciation, non-possessiveness, and celibacy.

Hinduism

Like Jains, **Hindus** believe in the transmigration upon rebirth into a human or animal form; however, unlike Jainism, according to Hindu theology, the effects of karma play a role in one's birth into the caste system and are controlled by a supreme being.

The earliest recorded beliefs about reincarnation come from India. Karma is an essential feature of Indian reincarnation beliefs where it is believed that every living being transmigrates (recycles) after death, carrying the seeds of karmic impulses into another life.

Karmic beliefs have evolved within the Hindu schools of thought. Some of the beliefs associated with karma are: it is a self-correcting mechanism, it binds beings to the cycle of births and deaths, it is caused by desires and the

The Cosmology of Reincarnation

activities of the senses, it is responsible for the evolution of beings from one stage to another, and that it is also possible to reverse karmic bondage. It is believed that just as a person incurs karma through his or her actions (including thoughts), collective karma occurs when nations, organizations, and associations incur karma because of collective actions and decisions.

Hinduism recognizes four types of karma operating in our lives simultaneously.

1. *Sanchita Karma* is the sum of the accumulated karma of previous lives.
2. *Prarabdha Karma* is that part of your Sanchita Karma currently activated in your present life, and which influences the course of your present life.
3. *Kriyamana Karma* is the karma whose consequences are experienced in this very life.
4. *Agami Karma* is the karma that arises out of your current life activities, whose consequences will be experienced by you in the coming lives.

Not all Hindu schools agree in the methods they recommend for dealing with the issue of karma, but they do agree that a major step is awareness of the law of karma, which is meant to be a corrective mechanism. When we realize that our thoughts, intentions, and actions cause our bondage and suffering, we become more discerning about what we do and how we live until we aim to lead divine-centered lives. In other words, living one's **dharma** is the path of righteousness. Righteous living or life on a dharmic path has four aspects: austerity/*tap*, purity/*shauch*, compassion/*daya*. and truthfulness/*satya*, according to the *Bhagavat Purana,* the revered text in Vaishnavism. The purpose of dharma is to attain a union of the soul with the supreme reality as well as to live by a code of conduct that is intended to secure both joy and happiness here and now on earth.

Buddhism

Like the Jains and Hindus, **Buddhists** believe actions from past lives affect the state of their current one and the actions that people take now will affect their future. According to Theravada Buddhist teacher Thanissaro Bhikkhu, most religions of India taught that karma operated in a simple straight line where past actions influence the present, and present actions influence the future. To Buddhists, karma is non-linear and complex. It acts in multiple feedback loops, with the present moment being shaped both by past and by present actions; present actions shape not only the future but also the present.

Jains believe that karma is an impure material or substance, which accumulates in the body and around the soul as an impurity according to one's actions. To be free from karma, Jains believe that one must physically remove that impurity through righteous actions, rigorous austerities, and self-purification. In contrast, Hindu and Buddhist traditions believe karma is an effect rather than a substance. The effects of karma are stored in the consciousness as latent impressions or subtle formations. They envision karma as an impure phenomenon or hidden effect and that the effects of karma must be resolved by addressing their causes.

In Buddhist communities, there is debate about anatta/no self and reincarnation versus rebirth. It can therefore be confusing when some Buddhists use words like soul and reincarnation. These concepts were clarified by Melanie Warner who wrote: "The Buddhist term for rebirth is *punabbhava*, which means 'again existence.' Buddhism sees rebirth not as the transmigration of a conscious entity but as the repeated occurrence of the process of existence. There is a continuity, a transmission of influence, a causal connection between one life and another. But there is no soul, no permanent entity which transmigrates from one life to another."[35]

From the Tibetan Buddhist perspective, the Dalai Lama said, "There are two ways in which someone can take rebirth after death: rebirth under the sway of karma and destructive emotions and rebirth through the power of compassion and prayer. Regarding the first, due to ignorance negative and positive karma are created and their imprints remain on the consciousness. These are reactivated through craving and grasping, propelling us into the next life. We then take rebirth involuntarily in higher or lower realms. This is the way ordinary beings circle incessantly through existence like the turning of a wheel. Even under such circumstances ordinary beings can engage diligently with a positive aspiration in virtuous practices in their day-to-day lives. They familiarize themselves with virtue that at the time of death can be reactivated providing the means for them to take rebirth in a higher realm of existence. On the other hand, superior Bodhisattvas, who have attained the path of seeing, are not reborn through the force of their karma and destructive emotions, but due to the power of their compassion for sentient beings and based on their prayers to benefit others. They can choose their place and time of birth as well as their future parents. Such a rebirth, which is solely for the benefit of others, is rebirth through the force of compassion and prayer."[36]

Gesha Choeden from the Drepung Gomang Monastery said that the effects of karma play out in three ways and each of these ways has subsets as follows:

1. Physical
    a. Murder
    b. Stealing
    c. Sexual misconduct
2. Speech
    a. Lying
    b. Speaking ill of others
    c. Harsh words
    d. Idle gossip
3. Mind
    a. Intense yearning/desire
    b. Angry/hurtful thoughts toward another
    c. Defaming another

The Cosmology of Reincarnation

For instance, the karma of someone who murders another could play out as a shorter life span while the karma of someone who steals could mean experiencing lack in another lifetime and needing to work hard.

The energy of one's actions, words, and thoughts accumulate in one's stream of consciousness and imprints on one's future. The accumulation of all of these can play out in the current life, the next life, or in another life. He said there are many schools of thought about where karmic information is stored, but the way to change one's karma is to refrain from negative actions, to do ones best to focus on positive actions such as following Buddhist's teachings. Recognizing that it takes practice, when one commits to right actions, especially the ones that concern the mind, one becomes compassionate and peaceful. He emphasizes the pragmatic applications in one's life including mundane aspects of life. (From talk at Sand Mandala Sacred Arts Tour at Hue Quang Temple, Nov. 22, 2023)

Karma is mutable; therefore, each moment is an opportunity to take positive action, to think positively, and to speak positively in a way that will lead us away from suffering. In other words, we can work with our karma to ensure a better future.

The differences between Jains, Hindus, and Buddhists are due to the differences in their understanding and interpretation of the nature of the world, creation, God, soul, reality, etc. These differences are hinted at here, but worth exploring further.

The Cosmology of Reincarnation

Taoism

Instead of reincarnation, **Taoists** use the term *Lun Hue*/transmigration cycle which means "return cycle" (*Lun*/wheel or cycle, *Hue*/return). Transmigration can occur in the human realm or other higher or lower realms. For Taoism, the Universe is the sum of three worlds: *Yu Jie* [yùjiè]/world of desire where all things are motivated and conditioned by the sensory effects, *See Jie* [shìjiè]/world of form where all things are subjugated by concrete and abstract shapes, and *See Wu Jie* [shìwújiè]/world of formlessness where there is no desire or form.

Each of the three worlds contains six "ways:"

1. Way of heaven, the realm of luminous deities.
2. Way of demons, the realm of obscure deities.
3. Way of man, the realm of human beings.
4. Way of animals, the realm of animals.
5. Way of the famished soul, the realm of souls obsessed with sensual desires.
6. Way of hell, the realm of suffering and illusion.

All beings in all six paths of all three worlds are subject to the laws of transmigration in which all beings are transformed through awareness of union with the Tao. In other words, Taoists' focus is not as much to end or stop the cycles of rebirth, but to follow the Tao and become one with Tao—the supreme principle that permeates the entire universe.[37]

Some Taoists' beliefs and practices are combined with Buddhism and/or shamanic beliefs and practices that use

Fourth century BCE Taoist philosopher, Zhuang Zhou (aka Chuang Tzu/Chuang Chou/Zhuangzi) said, "Birth is not a beginning; death is not an end. There is existence without limitation; there is continuity without a starting point. Existence with limitation is Space. Continuity without a starting point is Time. There is birth, there is death, there is issuing forth, there is entering in. That through which one passes in and out without seeing its form, that is the Portal of God."

"Taoism and Reincarnation: Why and How Does the Soul Return?"
Reincarnationafterdeath.com

rituals and such to transform energies that are not one with Tao.

Indigenous tribes

Most **Native American** tribes have strong beliefs about the existence of spirits, the afterlife, and reincarnation. Still other tribes such as the Lenape, the Western Shoshone, Goshute, Ute, Paiute, and Washoe do not believe in reincarnation at all.

According to Warren Jefferson, author of *Reincarnation Beliefs of North American Indians*, reincarnation is a central aspect of tribal cosmologies in these societies and their beliefs stem from their profound connection to their ancestors.

Among the North American cultures which include over five hundred tribes, some believe in animal-into-human and human-into-animal reincarnation, some as a natural evolution from insect to animal to human; however, others do not. Some have more complex views about and rituals for how souls reincarnate. Certain Native American tribes believe that one soul can incarnate into more than one body while some believe multiple people can share aspects of one soul. Others believe that one person can have two souls or have up to five souls in one body.

As animists, Native Americans believe that all things in nature, alive or inanimate, contain a spirit. When someone or something dies, they believe its spirit "passes over" and continues its existence in the spirit world. They view the natural and supernatural/spirit worlds as intrinsically linked.

The Cosmology of Reincarnation

Ideas about reincarnation are tied to the idea of a soul completing its purpose. For instance, if a person meets a sudden death, their soul cannot complete its journey on Earth. Thus, the soul must reincarnate until the journey is successfully completed. The same is true for someone who strays too far from their destined life path. The belief in the continuation of one's life purpose played a key role in the Amerindian way of life, according to Antonia Mills and Richard Slobodin, editors of *Amerindian Rebirth: Reincarnation Belief among North American Indians and Inuit*.

They describe such practices as:

1. Transmigration (human-to-animal and animal-to-human incarnations).
2. Multiple simultaneous reincarnation (aka divided reincarnation).
3. Marking the body of the deceased and watching for corresponding birthmarks in newborns.
4. Awareness of gender, which include considering a child a "two-spirit" (*niizh manidooway* in Ojibwa), transvestitism, and cross-sex identities, such as hermaphrodites or berdaches.
5. Recognizing a young child's connection with the spirit world, seeing their talents as memories from previous lives, and developing these in their naming customs: naming a newborn after a deceased relative because the baby is thought to be animated by or guided by that ancestor.

The Cosmology of Reincarnation

6. Child-rearing practices that recognize reincarnation beliefs.
7. Education that recognizes status and skills derived from a previous life.

The Southwestern Hopi's reincarnation belief system about karma resembles Hinduism and Buddhism where actions in this life have consequences that will be felt in subsequent lifetimes. Many tribes place a strong emphasis on proper burial as essential to liberate the soul so it can peacefully continue to the afterlife.

Ian Stevenson studied the reincarnation beliefs of the Tlingit people. They claimed to have learned these beliefs from individuals who had near-death experiences and from children who recalled events from the intermission period between incarnations. A Tlingit might choose to reincarnate to a certain family. Their spirits might announce their intentions in a dream or via an apparition. Newborns are checked for identifying physical marks, birthmarks, and birth defects. Reincarnation beliefs influence Tlingit naming customs, including giving a child multiple names when two or more spirits incarnate in a child or multiple children. "A child was expected to grow up to inherit other names, privileges, and statuses possessed by his namesake. Because these assets were [based on] lineage, clan and moiety property, a person could have again what he had before only if he made a suitable reincarnation and was given back his old name."[38]

The Cosmology of Reincarnation

Most Native American tribes have shamans, special members of a tribe or community who can communicate between the natural and supernatural worlds. Shamans use their gifts to discern information through their visions and bring these insights to their people through messages, stories, and even songs. They also use medicinal plants, such as psychoactive mushrooms, to facilitate vision quests and other spiritual trances. The shaman's wisdom forms the basis of the philosophical ideas and spiritual beliefs about souls, the afterlife, and reincarnation.

Mills and Slobodin documented comparable practices among Indigenous people worldwide, and Changzhen Li's book *100 Cases of Reincarnation Among the Dong People, a Study of the Dong Tribes of China* gives accounts similar to the Native American reincarnation beliefs, reinforcing the concept of migration of cultures and their beliefs.

African tribes

Although not widely realized, reincarnation is essential among many **African** religious systems and philosophies such as the Akamba (Kenya), Akan (Ghana), Lango (Uganda), Luo (Zambia), Ndebele (Zimbabwe), Sebei (Uganda), Yoruba (Nigeria), Shona (Zimbabwe), Nupe (Nigeria), and Illa (Zambia). Reincarnation is referred amongst the Yorubas of Nigeria in several ways, including *Yiya omo* ("shooting forth of a branch" or "turning to be child") and *A-tun-wa* ("another coming"). For the Aboh-speaking peoples of the Ibo family of nations in Nigeria,

The Cosmology of Reincarnation

Inua u'we is the "returning to life." They believe that death—an end to one life but also a gateway to another—is a spiritual necessity.[39]

There are varied understandings of the processes of rebirth. "Beliefs range from that in a 'partial' reincarnation of an ancestor in one or several individuals strictly within the same family, to that in an endless cycle of rebirths linked to a notion of cleansing and refinement of the inner nature." The Illa believe that a reincarnated spirit is sexless and may choose manifestation either as a man or woman and that the true Self provides no memory of the previous life to the newborn child.[40]

Andrew Rook compared the traditions of four African peoples of the composite nature of man with Theosophical doctrines.

Theosophy	Yoruba (Nigeria)	Nupe (Nigeria)	Illa (Zambia)	Lozi (Zambia)
Atman: spiritual essence	*Emin:* spiritual body	*Rayi:* life essence	*Moza* or *Muwo* "vital breath"	*Moyoo:* soul
Buddhi: compassionate nature	*Okan:* heart soul	*Kuci:* personal soul	*Mozo:* heart, will, intentions	*Mubiti* or *Situpu:* "envelope"
Manas: mind principle	*Iye:* mental body	*Fifingi:* "shadow"	*Shui* and *Rashimpulukutwi:* heart, soul, life principle	*Silumba:* double
Kama: desire principle	*Ojiji:* "shadow"	*Naka:* physical body	*Izhina:* "name" (lit.), personality	
Prana: vitality	*Ara:*		*Musedi*	

The Cosmology of Reincarnation

The Igbol (Nigeria) watch for birthmarks and behaviors to determine a child's previous life before naming him/her, but when no signs are apparent, they consult an oracle. Like the Tlingits, they believe it is possible to pre-plan one's reincarnation and to reincarnate in multiple bodies.[41]

Among the Yoruba (Nigeria), it is understood that an ancestor's *okan*/heart-soul seeks manifestation amongst his own descendants and the *emin*/spiritual body is the seat of life. In Nupe (Nigeria) tradition, the *kuci*/personal soul is said to animate the child of descendants at birth. "Nupe tribesmen illustrate the inevitability of the process of rebirth by comparing the journey of the kuci after death to the path of a stone thrown in the air: sooner or later it has to land somewhere!"[42]

The Akan people (Ghana) speak of rebirth as essential to reach one's full potential for compassion. In *The Akan Doctrine of God: A Fragment of Gold Coast Ethics and Religion*, Joseph B. Danquah writes, "It is like a man who dips a bucket in a deep well. The weight of the bucket when lifted up from the well would tell whether it is full of water or not. If it is felt to be light and not full, back down goes the bucket...until the weight assures the man the bucket is full. So is the soul's coming forth and going back into the source. He is not lifted up and taken into service with the source until his bucket of *nkrabea* (individual essence or destiny conferred by Nyankopan, an aspect of God) is completely filled with good—until the destiny of the soul is fully realized. And then it is a glad homegoing for the fully integrated soul. The return of a soul to earth is not therefore like a condemned criminal to be hanged, but more like a little child ready to learn more and to do better."[43]

Kabbalism

The **Kabbalistic** belief of **Gilgulum**—the revolving of souls through a succession of lives—goes back to the time of Moses. Rav Shimon bar Yochai said that the Creator conveyed revelations to Moses at Sinai and that a deep understanding of reincarnation was needed to comprehend them. [44]

Reincarnation is the key to penetrating the deep mysteries involved in *mitzvah of Yabim* (the obligation of the brother of a childless, deceased man to marry the widow) as well as all 613 mitzvot (commandments). If an individual does not succeed in fulfilling all mitzvot in one lifetime, one comes back again and again until finished. "Divine providence provides each person with the opportunities he needs to fulfill those particular mitzvot necessary for the perfection of his soul."[45]

Kabbalism is different from Buddhist doctrines about rebirth. Where Buddhists do not believe in a deity, the *Zohar*—a foundational work in the literature of Kabbalah— tells us that the Creator split each of us from Source, creating male and female. Each incarnation gives us an opportunity for *tikkun*, the correction of an aspect of himself, and whatever is incomplete is carried over into a future incarnation until the transformation is complete. The point is to be conscious of the things we have failed

Karmic retribution is not a feature of either the Jewish or Shia systems, but neither is the concept of penance before rebirth. Instead, God decides where to send souls to be reborn and judges them at the end of time, on the basis of the deeds of all their lives together.

> Elandur Haraldsson and James Matlock,
> *I Saw a Light and Came Here: Children's Experiences of Reincarnation*

The Cosmology of Reincarnation

at and make corrections accordingly. Awareness of our soul's journey guides our lives and helps us change and grow. Kabbalah teaches that we will reincarnate until we achieve complete transformation and eventually return to the source of all light, the Creator.[46]

People are given opportunities to exercise free will to transform karma. Humankind may incarnate into one of three lower kingdoms: animal, vegetable, and inanimate objects, depending on the nature of their negative activities. Eventually, we will pursue the path of examining our behaviors, and why we think the way we do. We will come closer to the purpose of our existence, the soul's journey back to the Light. We will develop a spiritual maturity that helps us perceive everything as part of a bigger picture and that death is not an end but a chance for a do-over. Kabbalah teaches us tools to understand the reincarnation process, to detect past life lessons, and how to gather the sparks of light back to itself. In her book *To Be Continued*, Karen Berg says that you can detect past life lessons by using kabbalistic tools of angels, astrology, palm reading, and face reading. The *Zohar* says that we carry *kilpot*, negative shells, of this incarnation but also from previous incarnations and the Creator prepares situations for us every day with the opportunity to make a correction that we need. When we make corrections in this life, it affects previous lives, and as we lift the shells, we move in the direction of the Creator.[47]

Like Buddhist bodhisattvas, some souls who complete the transformation return with a mission for humankind.

The Cosmology of Reincarnation

For example, Rav Shimon Bar Yochai, an "incarnated spark" of Moses, revealed the wisdom of the *Zohar*; and Ari, Rav Isaac Luria, an incarnated spark of Rav Shimom bar Yochai, appeared to interpret the *Zohar*. Ari states that if one does not understand the effect of prior lifetimes and how to make corrections for mistakes, this person will suffer the consequences. He says that reincarnation allows humankind to discover solutions to life's complexities.[48]

Rabbi Yonassan Gershom said that Jews prefer to reincarnate as Jews and within the same family if possible. He states that this concept is central to kabbalistic understanding of the Bible regarding the souls who were "standing at Sinai." These became and would remain Jewish for all incarnations, and that "rebirth into a non-Jewish body represents a very serious form of exile, a state of being literally 'cut off' (*karet*) from one's own people. On the other hand, a Gentile who converts to Judaism is seen as a lost soul on its way back home." Gershom said it is customary to whisper a person's Hebrew name into the ear of the deceased to prepare him/her to meet Dumah, the "Angel of the Grave," who meets the souls of the Jewish dead and asks for their Hebrew names. [49]

Rabbi Simon Jacobson says, "The ultimate goal, in a way, is creating a chain reaction where people, spirits, all over the world bond with one another, and we each allow our personal light to shine, and connect with the light of others. In Jewish faith this is the concept of Redemption, a personal redemption, a universal redemption, a world where spirituality is the priority and materialism is just a means toward an end." He says, "love is a continuous journey."[50]

The Cosmology of Reincarnation

Kabbalah teaches that what is true for the individual is also true for all humanity. When one person transforms, it affects the collective until critical mass creates a new world without suffering.

Druze

Plato's writings about the concepts of reincarnation influenced the **Druze's** tenets about reincarnation; however, their reincarnation beliefs state that a human soul will transfer only to a human body. As a closed system, community members are obligated to marry within the group and intermarriage is prohibited. Druze believe that upon death the soul immediately enters a newborn for another life, that a male Druze can be reincarnated only as another male Druze and a female Druze only as another female Druze; and that a Druze cannot be reincarnated in the body of a non-Druze.

The reincarnations continue until the "day of judgment" when the soul will be judged by its actions. Druze accept that people's behaviors can be influenced by a previous incarnation. Druze recognize signs of previous life memories appearing as difficulties in childhood—i.e., nervousness, discontent, fears, and longing for the previous family. When a child begins to mention details from a previous life, the family accepts the *nu☐q*—the phenomena of remembering and talking about a previous life. The person who remembers is called a *nā☐iq/nā☐iqa* (masculine/feminine).

It is common for Druze families to share their stories of remembering and to actively search for the corresponding previous family. Once found, a new order is created for the child and both families. *Nuṭq* often brings relief and if silenced, *nuṭq* remains like a "pain in the heart." *Nuṭq* is considered natural and part of a divine story. It is also common for details of the memories to fade in adulthood, but an aspect of the memory remains in the heart. Forgetfulness can lead to partial or full separation from the previous family, especially when the *nāṭiq/nāṭiqa* has his/her own family. The hierarchy between the two incarnations is toward the current one; however, it is acceptable to visit the previous incarnation's family at momentous events such as funerals or weddings. Even though *nuṭq* can create hardships initially, it is a cultural idiom which offers psychological and social resources. The *nuṭq* stories not only illustrate and reinforce the belief in reincarnation but also give evidence of the continuity of life.

Druze belief about the principle of rebirth—*taqammuṣ*—binds the community together, and the kinship ties created through *nuṭq* are a "gift of God."[51]

Theosophy

Theosophy was influenced by Madame Helena Blavatsky's search for wisdom. She traveled world-wide, studied Hinduism, Jainism, Sikhism, Buddhism, Egyptian mystery schools, shamanic cultures, and more. She co-created the Theosophical Society and formulated Theosophical beliefs, including beliefs about reincarnation which refer to a process in which the soul, once in the human form, never incarnates in an animal body. It continues with an idea of evolution of the Ego, or the Higher Ego/individual spiritual Monad, which appears throughout its cycles in various personalities. People incarnate in different circumstances according to the karma generated.

According to Blavatsky, "Karma is an Absolute and Eternal law in the World of manifestation... Karma is one with the Unknowable, of which it is an aspect in its effects in the phenomenal world."[52] Karma is infallible in its action, following the Law of Affinity which governs a relation between one's present situation in life and the actions one did in a past life as well as one's future existence.

Upon the death of the physical body, its "etheric double" (subtle energy body) usually moves on to the "astral plane" (the world of celestial spheres) where it relives its emotional life. Eventually, it goes through a second death and enters "devachan" (the dwelling place of the gods).

According to Theosophy, an entity's stay in devachan can last five hundred to one thousand years or more. There are, of course, exceptions to this general outline. For instance, when a person dies young, the process can be quite different, and rebirth can take place after a brief period. Also, the more consciousness is attached to physical life, the faster it will reincarnate.

Regardless, reincarnation gives us a greater sense of individual responsibility for our actions, knowing we cannot leave issues of prejudice, war, pollution, etc. to a future generation because we will be that future generation.

The Cosmology of Reincarnation

Rather than the idea of atonement, we must eventually pay for our own misdeeds.[53]

Harmony in the world of matter as it is in the world of spirit is the Theosophical decree of Karma. Human beings are destined to weave thread by thread around themselves, like a spider does his cobweb, to move through levels from the Lower/Personal "Ego," the Inner/Higher "Ego" (*Manas*), the Spiritual/Divine Ego (*Buddhi*), to the Higher Self (*Atma*). [Note that the Theosophical connotation of the word "Ego" refers to the sense of "I-ness" which can be expressed in the lower or higher Manas rather than the psychological term "ego."]

Blavatsky defines each of the levels in more detail as follows:

The Higher Self	Atma, the inseparable ray of the Universal and Oneself. It is the God above, more than within, us.
The Spiritual Divine Ego	The Spiritual soul of Buddhi, in close union with Manas, the mind-principle.
The Inner, or Higher "Ego"	Manas, the "Fifth" Principle. The Mind-Principle is only the Spiritual Ego when merged into one with Buddhi. It is the permanent Individuality or the "Reincarnating Ego."
The Lower, or Personal "Ego"	The physical man in conjunction with his lower Self

The subject of reincarnation and karma is complex. The law of karma applies equally to all, although all are not equally developed. In helping the development of others, the Theosophist believes that he is not only helping them fulfill their Karma, but he is also fulfilling his own, and the development of humanity. The key to development of oneself is through study, contemplation, conscious actions, and service.[54]

Anthroposophy

Anthroposophy grew as a spiritual movement when Rudolph Steiner broke away from the Theosophical Society in 1907 and created the Anthroposophical Society. While Theosophy was oriented toward an Eastern approach, Steiner adapted Theosophy's complex system and embraced a Christian path blended with natural science. However, he diverged from conventional Christian thought in several key places, such as reincarnation and karma. He chose the term anthroposophy (from Greek *anthropo*/human and *sophia*/wisdom) to emphasize humanity's wisdom. He wanted to utilize the scientific method to develop the process of inner development to bring new truths to humanity without the dogma of past religious systems. He believed as human consciousness evolved, the understanding of reincarnation advanced one's connection between the physical and spiritual world. Moral impulses would follow and affect relationships and every aspect of one's life. Steiner said past life memories are "sentient impressions in the life of Soul." Realizing that not everyone remembered their previous lives, he focused on ways to contemplate one's life and to live consciously.

Steiner developed exercises in his book *How to Know Higher Worlds* to develop higher levels of consciousness through meditation and observation, and to guide the spiritual in the human being to the spiritual in the universe. To apply anthroposophical teachings, the Anthroposophical Society created the Waldorf education system; biodynamic agriculture (the first intentional organic farming movement); anthroposophical medicine, including homeopathic remedies; Sonnenhof and Camphill Movement schools focused on special needs education; and organic architecture. Through developing socially responsible finance and entrepreneurship, counseling services, and artistic expression, Anthroposophy continues to have an impact on social reform.

Channeled teachings about reincarnation

Today there are a myriad of **"channelers,"** but for this book, we will focus on a few of the ground-breaking channelers and what they taught about reincarnation. The entities who were channeled are often a group of entities rather than an individual person. They range from beings who have incarnated but no longer need to reincarnate in the physical form to entities who have not incarnated. However, they choose to assist humankind in a different form or frequency. Some entities are highly evolved beings from other worlds. The channeled teachings are presented here as *something to consider*, but as with all the previous information, it is up to the reader to discern what resonates as truth to you. As we explore the outer reaches of our Universe with instruments such as the James Webb telescope, we are faced with the question: Is there sentient life out there? Are these channelers giving us another "Copernican moment" when we must reevaluate everything that we thought we knew?

Seth, who was channeled by Jane Roberts from the 1960s–1980s, said, "Since all is simultaneous, your present beliefs can alter your past ones, whether from this life or a 'previous' one...you can restructure your 'reincarnational past' in the same way that you can restructure the past in this present life."[55] He said that one's other lives are unconsciously aware of your conscious experience, as you are unconscious of theirs. This applies to the "future" as well as "past" lives. Each reincarnational entity has many probable lives and the whole of all one's reincarnational selves is changed by each of its comprehensions. Each is a portion of the other as a city is part of a state, or an individual is part of a family. In fact, there is a great interchange of information with all one's selves, but it is easier for changes to occur in certain cycles.

Seth encourages you to employ your imagination constructively to alter past, present, and future. Imagination follows your beliefs and creates your physical reality. Working with your imagination acts as a trigger drawing information from other levels of reality, creating alternate probabilities. The process reaches into deep biological structures at which point the "probabilities are altered, and the condition erased in your present—but also in your past."[56]

At every point you have free will. The present is your point of focus, power, and action. Therefore, Seth recommends practicing daily, concentrating on using your imagination, and your current beliefs will reprogram. According to Seth, death is one night to the soul. He said, "Each part is vital, and in one way or another there is instant communication between the smallest and the largest, the cobweb and the spider, the man, the entity, and the star—and each spins its own web of probabilities from which other universes continually spin."[57] The first step is to enlarge your beliefs.

Seth says using hypnosis can help you discover the source of old patterns and facilitate change to help you be in your point of power in the present. Seth said, "there is no karma to be paid off as punishment unless you believe that there are crimes for which you must pay."[58]

The **Michael Teachings** began in the 1970s when a group of people in the San Francisco Bay Area, including Sarah and Richard Chamber, Eugene Trout, and others, got together over a Ouija board and began channeling an entity of one thousand and fifty beings who identified as Michael. They created a study group to learn more about the new spiritual teaching based in love, documented the teachings, and shared them to help others become more of who they truly are—essences/aspects of Tao.[59]

According to the Michael Teachings, our souls are sparks of consciousness from Tao that manifest into the physical world.[60] Philip Wittmeyer's *History of the Overleaf*

The Cosmology of Reincarnation

Chart[61] gives details about the types of souls (infant, baby, young, mature, old, transcendental, and infinite) and about the roles (warrior, server, artisan, scholar, sage, priest, and king). He explains the Michael Teachings' categories of goals, attitudes, chief features, modes, and attributes as well as the contributions by many who have channeled the Michael group.

The only requirement is that the soul completes the experiential levels of the five soul age stages and the accompanying internal monads (units of experiences). Karma is the soul's means of "checks and balances," creating a karmic debt that is owed to another as an energetic imbalance between two or more souls that need to be rebalanced. The karmic debt does not need to be in the form of an eye for an eye. Karma is a learning experience. You learn from the choices you make, and you learn that choices have consequences. [62]

Caris Palm Turpen's *7 Levels of Karmic Debt* describes a fascinating process of balancing energies through the levels:

1. Ice Cream Debt/Simple Exchange.
2. Toolbox Debt/Support or Interruption of Daily Flow.
3. Prized Automobile Debt/Emotional Attachments
4. Heart and Home Debt/Personal Power
5. Livelihood Debt/Expression
6. Integrity Debt.
7. Personal Knowingness Debt.[63]

Chelsea Quinn Yarbro, author of *Messages from Michael* (1979), sums it up when she said that life is the meaning of existence and is our teacher to develop self-acceptance and tolerance toward others.[64]

The Law of One, also known as the **RA Material,** developed from one hundred and six lessons channeled by Carla Rueckert from RA—a sixth density social memory complex that originated from Venus 2.6 billion years ago. These sessions were recorded by Don Elkins between 1981 and 1984. Aaron Abke summarizes the RA teachings as follows: "There's one being in the Universe experiencing itself in fragments and bringing those experiences back to the One...All is one and that one is love/light, light/love, the Infinite Creator."[65] There are seven densities which are not a dimension in space and time but a non-local stage of Soul, a frequency of Soul. The seven densities, from lower to higher, include: elements, animals, humans, light body beings, the path to wisdom, and the Creator. Reincarnation gives an entity opportunities to awaken to Self. The purpose of the third density is to choose what happens through self-awareness in the context/environment of forgetting. Such awareness leads to a stage of "harvest" (graduation into the density/vibrations most comfortable to them).[66] According to RA, harvests occur after each twenty-five thousand year "major cycle" as well as at the end of a complete seventy-five thousand year "master cycle." The harvest process is facilitated by angelic presences, members of the Confederation of Planets, and guardians from the next octave of Creation.[67]

The Cosmology of Reincarnation

When asked "How did humans come about?" RA replied, "Our Logos [Creative Principle or Love], in its plan for how best to allow the Creator to know itself, chose to invest bipedal apes with self-consciousness."[68] (90.12) By developing speech, rather than telepathy, the human experiencers would, through free will, eventually remember the path back to the Creator and therefore become jewels in the crown of the Creator.[69]

Sanaya Roman (1949–2021) studied at the University of California at Berkeley. She also studied metaphysics, the Seth books by Jane Roberts, and the Alice Bailey books. She began channeling **Orin**, a being of light who exists in the same dimension as our Higher Selves. Part of his purpose is to assist us in being our Higher Selves. Sanaya and Orin wrote the Earth Life series (*Living with Joy*, *Personal Power Through Awareness*, and *Spiritual Growth*) to guide humanity through a time of major transition and awakening. Their *Opening to Channel* book walks you through the channeling process. Their books and courses offer ways to transcend karmic energies, to grow spiritually, and to choose the reality you want to experience. Their teachings are less convoluted than the Seth Material, the Michael Teachings, and the Law of One. According to Orin, "They will help you awaken to the multidimensional being you are, tap into the greater plan of humanity's evolution, and discover the part you came to play in these wonderful, exciting times of transformation."

What are you here to do? Recognizing life purpose manifests your destiny. Do not get me wrong; you are free beings. You did not set out a course before you were born that you had to follow. You laid some groundwork, provided yourself with certain parents, and chose to be born in a certain part of the world. You set up circumstances for your life so you would be aimed like a projectile in a certain direction. Once you are here, your life is absolutely spontaneous and decided upon from moment to moment.

Sanaya Roman, *Living with Joy*

The Cosmology of Reincarnation

A Scientific Approach

The Department of Perceptual Studies (DOPS) at the University of Virginia has collected data for over fifty years of more than twenty-five hundred cases of children who claim to remember previous lives. Dr. Ian Stevenson founded UVA DOPS in 1967 with the financial assistance of Chester Carlson, the founder of xerography. Dr. James Tucker is the current director.

These cases of the reincarnation type (CORT) involve children often around two to three years old. Some cases (CORT-I) include memories of the intermission between incarnations. The research indicates that children who remember previous lives:

1. Show behavior that is unusual in the child's family, but appropriate for the previous family, such as likes and dislikes for people, food, clothing, etc.
2. Show phobias corresponding to the mode of death in the previous life.
3. Exhibit unusual play that reenacts a vocation/profession, parenting skills, or the mode of death of a previous personality.[70]

Intermission memories (CORT-I) fall into four categories: memories of the previous personality's funeral, memories of events from the previous personality's life, memories of an existence in another realm, and memories of conception or birth. CORT-I accounts describe three stages. The first stage is a transitional stage where the subject might see the preparation of the previous personality's body, the funeral, or the grieving relatives, only to find that they cannot communicate with them. This state often ends when the subject is directed by an elder to the next state. The second state varies from living in a location to having specific tasks to do, and sometimes interacting with other discarnate personalities. The final stage is one of preparing for the next incarnation including choosing or being directed to one's parents. Intermission memories are comparable to Near Death Experiences (NDEs) with reports of mystical beings and meeting other discarnate beings.[71]

Dr. Ian Stevenson's and Dr. Jim Tucker's scientific research at DOPS have added volumes to the evidence suggestive of reincarnation. They are not alone as others join this field of study.

Revelations from Regression Therapy

While reincarnation research such as the cases collected at DOPS/UVA give us a scientific perspective, the evidence gathered from Past Life Regressions shows us a therapeutic point of view where the focus is to assist the subject's process.

In shamanic practices, the shaman was the seer and healer. Today, the Past Life Regression Therapist is the *guide* empowering the subject on his/her journey of integrating aspects of consciousness. Past Life Regression cases continue to expand upon what ancient sages experienced and taught. Today, a growing interest in and development of Past Life Regression Therapy (PLRT), Life between Life (LBL), and Quantum Consciousness Experience (QCE), coupled with the technological evolution of worldwide communication, has significantly expanded our knowledge of reincarnation. The expansion of consciousness is growing exponentially, but what has the therapeutic point of view learned from its experience?

Cases from past life regressions, life-between-life sessions, and quantum consciousness experiences show us that we are sojourners through many lands, nationalities, cultures, and belief systems. We can choose many forms, genders, and types of experiences, and no matter what we choose, the overriding lesson is about love. Not everyone who journeys in a regression experiences the reunion with Oneness/Source; however, the ones who do share their stories which are reminiscent of those of mystics and near-death experiencers.

The information collected by physician and regression therapist Joel Whitton gives us many accounts of his subjects' interlife experiences. He said, "The environment of the life between life is a reflection of each person's thought forms and expectations." They describe a wide variety of landscapes between incarnations, from palaces, gardens, temples, schools, abstract planes, to a brilliant euphoric energy of light. "Those who are keen to proceed vigorously with their spiritual development tend to be most consciously active between incarnations. Those who show little interest in the evolutionary process are inclined to 'sleep' for the equivalent of huge tracts of earthbound

Before a man studies Zen, to him mountains are mountains and waters are waters. After he gets an insight into the truth of Zen, through the instruction of a good master, mountains are not mountains and waters are not waters. After this, when he really attains to the abode of rest, mountains are once more mountains and waters are waters.

Roger J. Woolger, Ph.D., *Other Lives, Other Selves: A Jungian Psychotherapist Discovers Past Lives* time...To enter meta consciousness is to be one with the timeless oversoul which is the invisible cornerstone of the powers of the individual."[72]

Whitton's subjects tell of an indescribable language of telepathic communication that is difficult to translate into words or even into symbols. He says that under hypnosis an entity can possess greater self-awareness than it would have in ordinary consciousness, and that human emotions are shed except in rare cases while "cognitive emotions" are maintained in the astral/subtle body. The "life review" is the entity's decisive moment where wise beings (highly advanced spiritual beings who may have completed their cycle of earthly incarnations) radiate restorative, healing energy, and assurance that all experiences happen for a reason. They assist the entity in evaluating the life just passed, objectively understanding one's spiritual journey, and make recommendations concerning the next incarnation.

The "life review" is like climbing into a movie of one's life with complete instantaneous sensory detail where the entity intuitively absorbs meaning from this experience beyond the replayed scenes. The knowledge gained prepares the entity for the decisions that will determine its next incarnation, often with guidance from the wise beings who are mindful of its karmic lessons. Recommendations are made according to the entity's needs and a plan is made. Occasionally, an entity rejects the recommendations, but that is his/her choice even though the consequences may be more challenging.

The entity passes through a stage to lower the vibrations of its consciousness before reentering the Earth plane, a necessary step to subjugate memories of the interlife experience to evaluate what one has learned. "One fundamental aspect the privileged few who have visited the interlife receive [is] the same unrelenting message: *We are thoroughly responsible for who we are and the circumstances in which we find ourselves. We are the ones who do the choosing.*"[73]

Jungian analyst and past life therapist Roger Woolger suggests three stages of understanding the reincarnation process:

1. Realistic/cathartic stage—the linear cause-and-effect sequence means a literal perspective.
2. Symbolic/archetypal stage—we move from identifying with the other life to sorting out the influence of other selves as an observer into "the transcendent function." The split part is healed; the shadow is integrated through love and acceptance. In this stage, we see that all people are reflections of our inner shadow and our light through compassion and grace.
3. Integral/mystical stage—glimpses of a greater pattern shift one's perspective, moving beyond all opposites. At the integral/mystical level of consciousness, all other lives are aspects of Self. All are both one and many.

Data from regressions indicate karmic lessons and/or balancing rather than retribution. Life-between-life/intermission experiences show us compassionate guidance rather than a day of judgment. The lessons and experiences lead us to reunion with the Source and the sense of wonder about our individual purpose in each incarnation as well as our contribution to the collective. The data also shows a myriad of possibilities such as parallel lives, alternate realities, split souls/multiple simultaneous incarnations, soul aspects/fragments, and multiverses. This often leaves us with more questions than answers, but is it possible that that is part of the Divine Plan? If the overriding lesson is about love, is it possible that the never-ending journey, whether on Earth or elsewhere, *is* our goal and that our lives are, as Dr. Raymond Moody suggests, "God's stories"?

3 THE EVOLUTION OF REGRESSION THERAPY

If indeed Ian Stevenson was correct about Tlingits' reincarnation beliefs descended from Siberian ancestors, what can we discern about the ability of some traditional healers and shamans to communicate with ancestors and spirits to help their people heal beyond time?

Ancient shamanic healing practices also impacted Hindu, Buddhist, Taoist, and other tribal beliefs in Asia and the South Pacific. Each group contains members who have gifts in specific areas such as communicating with spirits, ancestors, or remembering past lives. Does this correlate to the small percentage of the current population of psychic/mediums who remember their lives? For now, this is a thought exercise based on observation and deduction, but it leads us to the zig-zag trail from early shamanic practices to the evolution of hypnotherapy and past life regression therapy.

Hypnotherapy is a therapeutic technique that uses hypnosis to shift the subject's state of consciousness to allow focused concentration. Past Life Regression Therapy is a therapeutic technique that uses hypnosis and guided meditation, often in combination with other healing modalities such as Reiki and EFT (Emotional Freedom

Technique), to recall past lives, and regression therapy also focuses on the past of the current life.

The shaman's role has evolved. As a modern-day shaman, the therapist guides the subject through his/her journey or experience and may or may not share the experience with the subject. One need not interpret the images as actual past lives nor believe in the concept of reincarnation to benefit from Past Life Regression Therapy.

The use of hypnotherapy and Past Life Regression Therapy goes back thousands of years and as you will see recent discoveries have contributed to their evolution.

Sleep Temples 2000 BCE, Early Hypnosis

Over four thousand years ago, **Sleep temples** (also known as **dream temples** or **Egyptian sleep temples**) were some of the early examples of hypnosis. They were healing sanctuaries where patients rested in an unlit chamber and listened to chanting to enter a trance-like state. Before falling into this state, they were given suggestions to call to the gods for assistance with their dreams. The dreams were analyzed and treatments (meditation, fasting, baths, and offerings of sacrifices to the deities or spirits) were suggested. The suggestions helped cast out bad spirits affecting the person's mind and body.

Similar healing centers existed for practitioners in the Middle East, Ancient Greece, and in the Jewish culture. In 1928, a Roman sleep temple was discovered at Lydney Park, Gloucestershire by Mortimer Wheeler.

David Reeves said, "Æsclepius (also spelt: Asclepios, Æsclepius, Æsculapius, Æsclepius) was a healer, his mythical roots going back in to the second millennium BCE, he became a demi-god. Over time he evolved into a temple god in his own right. The temples in his honor were temples of healing dreams. His daughters were Hygea and Panacea. A Klíně was a sacred place, or a sacred skin set out around the temple, where the sick person reclined to enter the dream state. From these names we have derived the words, Panacea, Hygiene and Clinic."[74]

The earliest known teachings about Past Life Regression can be traced back to around 2500 years ago in Pythagoras' mystery school where he taught esoteric subjects, including how to remember one's past life/lives. It is not clear whether the techniques were continued or not.

Did others stumble on past life memories just as contemporary pioneers in the field? Or was it just a matter of time before humans would be ready to accept, embrace, and utilize Past Life Regression as a therapeutic practice? From what is known about others who developed their own modalities, regression therapy has gone through an evolutionary process.

From Animal Magnetism/Mesmerism to Hypnosis

In the eleventh century CE, a Persian physician **Avicenna (Ibn Sina**, 980–1037), author of the *Book of Healing*, wrote about the distinction between sleep and *al-Wahm al-Amil* (hypnosis) versus animal magnetism, an invisible natural force possessed by all living things, including humans, animals, and vegetables. While **Paracelus** (1493–1541) was the first physician to use magnets in his practice, he protested Avicenna's untested methods by burning the latter's books.

The Irish faith healer **Valentine Greatrakes** (1628–1682) who practiced "laying on of hands," and Viennese Jesuit **Maximilian Hell** (1720–1792), who was interested in healing with magnets, set the stage for **Franz Anton Mesmer** (1734–1815) who was known for his work with animal magnetism/mesmerism, a force/power in the bodies of animals, including humans. Mesmer created a manual about the phenomena and practices of animal magnetism, laying the foundation for healing practices to follow. They include twenty-six properties that pose the idea that a responsive relationship exists between the heavenly bodies, the earth, and all animated bodies. This relationship is analogous to magnetic forces. It is like light and is communicated by sound. Mesmer proposed that these principles would cure nervous diseases directly, and other diseases indirectly, and will enable the physician to decide upon the health of every individual.[75]

Mesmer faced criticism of his work by other physicians and was kicked off the faculty at the University of Vienna and later forbidden to practice medicine in Vienna. Yet, he was popular with the French aristocracy and his theory attracted a wide following by some medical communities. He stated, "To the physical causes of disease must be added

The great object in all these processes is to induce a habit of abstraction or concentration of attention, in which the subject is entirely absorbed with one idea, or train of ideas, whilst he is unconscious or indifferently conscious to every other object, purpose, or action.

James Braid

moral causes: pride, ambition, all the vile passions of the human mind, are as many causes of visible maladies."[76]

Serge Kahili King summed up Mesmer's contributions, "Mesmer's many experiments and successful results were also proof that he was working with an actual transference of energy of some type."[77]

It was a follower of Mesmer, **Etienne Felix d'Henin de Cuviller**, who practiced mesmerism and in 1820 coined the term "hypnotism," from neuro-hypnotism (nervous sleep).

Another student of Mesmer, **Marquis de Puysegur** (1751–1825), was recognized as one of the pre-scientific founders of hypnotism. He identified the difference between sleeping trance (what he called artificial somnambulism and is now called hypnosis) and natural sleepwalking (somnambulism). He observed what happened to a person while in trance, particularly how a person's symptoms and behavior could be influenced by the facilitator and focused on a subject-centered treatment.

Joseph-Claude-Anthelme Recamier (1774–1852) was the first physician to use hypno-anesthesia during operations.

James Braid (1795–1860), the Scottish neurosurgeon, expanded on Mesmer's ideas. In 1842, he popularized the term "hypnosis," and is credited with writing the first book on hypnosis, *Neurypnology* (1843). He earned the title as the "Father of Modern Hypnotism." He studied Asian meditation techniques after reading the Persian text *Dabistan-I Mazahib* and learning about the ability to self-hypnotize.

He saw meditation and yoga as precursors to hypnosis. Rejecting Mesmer's idea that hypnosis was induced by magnetism, Braid ascribed the "mesmeric trance" to a physiological process resulting from prolonged attention to moving objects or similar object of fixation.

In 1834, **Dr. John Elliotson** (1791–1868), an English surgeon, reported numerous painless surgical operations that had been performed using mesmerism, and founded a hospital for the use of hypnosis in surgical operation. **Dr. James Esdaile** (1805–1859) reported on 345 major operations performed using mesmeric sleep as the sole anesthetic in British India.

In the early 1800s, **Abbe Faria/Jose Custodio de Faria**, an Indo-Portuguese priest, introduced "oriental hypnosis," an Indian practice of self-hypnosis or trance states created by rhythmic breathing exercise and meditation and using a focused stare and suggestive commands to "sleep" when working with others. He claimed that hypnosis was generated from within the mind by the power of suggestion or expectancy and cooperation of the subject, not the facilitator. Therefore, he emphasized suggestion and demonstrated the existence of "autosuggestion." Faria pioneered scientific study of hypnosis with an emphasis on the connection of hypnosis with the mind, a concept that led **Hippolyte Bernheim** and **Ambriose-Auguste Liebeault** to establish the Nancy school (Nancy, France) dedicated to therapeutic hypnosis in the 1860s.

Jean-Martin Charcot (1825–1893) followed in Faria's footsteps endorsing hypnotism for hysteria. He used a process of post-hypnotic suggestion. His pupil **Pierre Janet** used hypnotherapy for dissociative personalities, the splitting of mental aspects, and explored the subconscious to help patients with reintegration therapy.

Meanwhile, Russian physicians used obstetric hypnosis. **Ferdinand Lamaze** (1891–1957), who visited Russia, brought back to France a method for childbirth without pain using hypnosis.

The use of hypnosis merged with psychiatry in World War I and II and the Korean War for use of what is now known as Post Traumatic Stress Disorder.

Hypnosis and hypnotherapy were gaining acceptance. The British Medical Association endorsed hypnosis for therapeutic use in 1892, but medical schools and universities were not quick to recognize it. By 1955, the British Medical Association approved the use of hypnosis in psychoneuroses and hypno-anesthesia for pain management in childbirth and surgery and advised training in hypnosis for physicians and medical students.

In 1958, the American Medical Association approved medical uses of hypnosis and in 1960, the American Psychological Association endorsed hypnosis as a branch of psychology.

In 2003, the Indian Ministry of Health and Family Welfare approved the use of hypnotherapy within the medical profession and in 2006 the Academy of Family Physicians of Malaysia accredited hypnotherapy training.

The Roman Catholic Church had banned hypnotism until 1956 when Pope Pius XII approved hypnosis as a treatment by health care professionals when following medical guidelines.

The twentieth century was a time of rapid evolution of hypnosis processes.

The Coué method, developed by French pharmacist **Émile Coué** (1857–1926), centered on the promotion of conscious autosuggestion through an ordered sequence of rational, systematic, hypnotherapeutic interactions that are subject-centered. Coué stressed the significance of both unconscious and conscious autosuggestion blended with common-sense explanations and experiential exercises. Coué encouraged ego-strengthening statements practiced daily such as "Every day, in every way, I'm getting better and better."

Ericksonian Hypnosis has influenced many modern schools of hypnosis. **Milton Erickson** (1901–1980), an American psychiatrist and psychologist who specialized in medical hypnosis and family therapy, was the founding president of the American Society of Clinical Hypnosis. He inspired a renaissance of hypnosis with his techniques—strategic family therapy, family systems therapy, solution focused brief therapy, and neuro-linguistic programming—focusing on the unconscious mind as creative and solution-generating. Four volumes of his seminars, workshops, and lectures were compiled in *Healing in Hypnosis* (1983), *Life Reframing in Hypnosis* (1984), *Mind-Body Communication* (1987), and *Creative Choice in Hypnosis* (1992).

One of the pioneers of the medical use of hypnosis was **Dave Elman** (born David Kopelman in 1900). He became interested in hypnosis when a family friend rapidly relieved Elman's father's pain from cancer with hypnosis. He was determined to learn these techniques. Although not a doctor or psychotherapist, he taught countless doctors, dentists, therapists, and anesthesiologists his methods to induce trance and help find the root cause of problems once people were in the altered state. Elman defined hypnosis "as a state of mind in which the critical faculty of the subject is bypassed, and selective thinking is established." He traveled the U.S. teaching hypnosis to doctors and dentists in his "Medical Relaxation" series. In 1964, he published *Findings in Hypnosis*.

Fast forward to the twenty-first century. "Hypnosis is no longer a debatable 'Is this stuff real?' issue," said Karl Smith, author of *Hypnosis or Hypnotherapy*. He points to brain imaging and brain scans showing the efficacy of hypnosis and hypnotherapy. In 2000, Stanford University's study used a PET (Positron Emission Tomography) scanner to show the areas of the brain activated during hypnosis.

David Spiegel, M.D. said, "Hypnosis is the oldest Western form of psychotherapy...it's a very powerful means of changing the way we use our minds to control perception and our bodies."[78]

In 2008, researchers led by Richard J. Davison, director of the Waisman Lab for Brain Imaging and Behavior at the University of Wisconsin-Madison, learned that the brain changes (a phenomena referred to as neuroplasticity) when Tibetan monks meditated with a focused intention.[79]

An MRI (Magnetic Resonance Imaging) study at Stanford published in 2016 showed parts of the brain that function differently under hypnosis, and an EEG (electroencephalogram) showed changes in neural patterns in the brain under hypnosis. The hypnosis process showed a significant decrease in the area called the dorsal anterior cingulate part of the brain's salience network; and an increase in connections between the dorsolateral prefrontal cortex and the insula—the brain-body connection that helps the brain process and control what is going on in the body.[80]

From Hypnosis to Past Life Regression Therapy

Past life regression therapy grew out of hypnotherapy, often serendipitously. Psychologists, psychiatrists, and other medical practitioners were key participants. Although they were often met with condemnation, the results were undeniable.

Could past life regression therapy (PLRT) be the beginning of understanding consciousness in a new way? Could PLRT be a bridge between ordinary consciousness and metaconsciousness? Metaconsciousness is a concept described by Joel Whitton as an intense awareness of personal identity merged with existence itself to learn the reason for being. It transcends personal karma. Language and symbols cannot capture its essence.[81]

The Cosmology of Reincarnation

In the fifth century BCE, **Pythagoras** taught his students the concepts of metempsychosis, the process where the mind transmigrates or to put it another way, where a unit of consciousness (our divine identity) takes different forms to experience a variety of characteristics within the field of creation. He advocated vegetarianism. He taught his students to remember by bringing their awareness to the events of the day, the week, and so forth until they recalled previous existences.[82]

Buddhaghosha (fifth century CE) gave explicit instructions in *Vishuddhi Marga (Path of Purity)* to his fellow Buddhists about how to retrieve past life memories by meditating deeply on recent events. Then, he suggests remembering a full day's events and continue remembering further back until one remembers the moment of death in the previous life. He says that once the previous existence has been retrieved, others are easier to remember.[83]

Did others explore memories about past lives therapeutically? The records are incomplete until the early twentieth century CE.

English occultist **Aleister Crowley's** (1875–1947) reputation gained him fame and notoriety. His contribution in regression therapy was to coin the word "Magical Memory" for one's past life memories. He recommended using a rigorous procedure like Buddhaghosha's to attain magical memory details which should then be thoroughly cross-checked. In his book *Magick in Theory and Practice* (1929), he said, "Genuine recollections almost invariably explain oneself to oneself." He added, "Anything which throws light upon the Universe, anything which reveals us to ourselves, should be welcome in this world of riddles."

A.R. (Asa Roy) Martin (1887–1949) was an ordained Coptic teacher who is noted as the first person to do Past Life Regression in the U.S. He formed a study group to develop his technique and published his findings in *Researches in Reincarnation and Beyond* (1942).

British psychiatrist **Sir Alexander Cannon**'s *The Power Within* (1953) summarized one thousand sessions to show the connection between past and present lives.[84]

Morey Bernstein (1920–1999) learned hypnosis from Jerry Thomas in the 1940s, but it was the *Reincarnation Outflanks Freud* chapter in Sir Alexander Cannon's book *The Power Within* that caught his attention. When he met Virginia Tighe in 1952 and recorded her memories of Bridey Murphy, an Irish woman who lived in the 1800s, in his book *The Quest for Bridey Murphy* (1956), he created quite a sensation. It sparked "come as you were" parties, songs, and movies, but research about Tighe's memories showed they were fraught with discrepancies and created controversy about hypnosis.

Helen Wambach, Ph.D. (1925–1985) vividly recalled details of a spontaneous past life memory when she visited a Quaker Memorial in 1966. Shocked by the experience and aware of the Bridey Murphy scandal, she was determined to do solid research to understand her personal encounter. Ten years of over two thousand regression sessions with her subjects changed her life and the direction of her work as an innovative therapist. She became one of the first great researchers in past and future lives focusing on tabulating details from hundreds of subjects in specific time periods. She shared her findings in her books *Life Before Life* (1979) and *Reliving Past Lives: The Evidence Under Hypnosis* (1978).

In her book *You Have Been Here Before; a Psychologist Looks at Past Lives* (1978), **Edith Fiore, Ph.D.** (1930–) opened the door a little further to the concept of reincarnation. Her books *The Unquiet Dead: A Psychologist Treats Spirit Possession* (1995) and *Encounters* (1997) went further out on the limb to explore spirit attachments and contacts with extraterrestrials.

Like so many others, **Dolores Cannon** (1931–2014) "accidentally" stumbled upon reincarnation in the 1960s. She and her husband Johnny, who had both trained in hypnosis for weight loss and smoking cessation, were consulted by a doctor at the naval base where Johnny was stationed to help one of his patients. The woman suffered from a nervous eating disorder, was extremely obese, had high blood pressure, and suffered from kidney problems. Midway through the session, the woman unexpectedly began describing scenes from a past life where she was a flapper living in Chicago in the roaring twenties. They watched as the woman transformed into a different personality with different vocal patterns and body mannerisms. They decided to go with the flow of the session and see what they could find out. Over the next several months, Dolores and Johnny regressed the woman through five different and distinct lifetimes back to when

God created her. The story is told in *Five Lives Remembered* (2009).

After conducting sessions with thousands of clients, recording the results, and spending significant time and energy to verify the authenticity of her clients' past lives, Dolores concluded she had tapped into an incredibly powerful source of information. After developing and refining her technique over many years, Dolores established Quantum Healing Hypnosis Technique□ (QHHT) to enable direct communication with the subconscious for answers to any question. She developed a training course for QHHT and wrote many books about her experiences, including *The Convoluted Universe* (five volumes, 2001–15), and *The Three Waves of Volunteers and the New Earth* (2011).

In the 1960s, **Morris Netherton** (1935–2020) sought help for ulcers and dermatitis. His psychotherapist took him into an age regression where he experienced a past life that was connected to his dermatitis. His career as a therapist began to shift. As a supervising counselor with the Los Angeles Probation Department, he honed his skills as his subjects recalled prenatal, birth, past lives, and traumatic experiences. He developed past life therapy protocol and published his techniques in *Past Lives Therapy* (1978) with N. Shiffrin.

Another pioneer who helped shape thoughts about past lives was **Dick Sutphen** (1937–2019). His books *You Were Born Again to Be Together* (1976) and *Past Lives, Future Loves* (1978) paved the way for mainstream acceptance of reincarnation in Western culture. He regressed thousands and gathered theories about reincarnation from their experiences. He theorized that each soul was bound in a "soul matrix" linking a series of past, present, or future lives and that karma is an "unerring universal law." He said that each soul may have three or four simultaneous or overlapping lives comparable to Seth's concept of an *eternal now*, a "timeless" present in which the past, present, and future exist simultaneously (Jane Roberts). Sutphen led his subjects into their "superconscious" mind. They viewed their experiences from a timeless perspective where all lives are active and alive concurrently. Only when the perspective shifts to a specific life does the continuum collapse into the local space/time condition represented in an individual incarnation. He theorized that each soul is a creator generating a tree of soul associations.[85]

William J. Baldwin D.D.S., Ph.D. (1939–2004) started out in dentistry and used hypnosis in his practice. However, after experiencing spontaneous past life memories in the late 1970s, he explored Past Life Regression Therapy. Inspired by Dr. Edith Fiore's spirit releasement work, he trained with Fiore and with Morris Netherton, and left his dentistry practice to study clinical psychology. His dissertation was entitled *Diagnosis and Treatment of the Spirit Possession Syndrome* which became the subject of his book *Spirit Releasement Therapy: A Technique Manual* (1991). He integrated pastoral counseling and psychology with a wide range of techniques to illuminate the foggier borders between subpersonalities, ancestral spirits, multiples, possessing entities, and past life selves.

"*Metaconsciousness is a supremely paradoxical state of memory awareness in which the percipient loses all sense of personal identity by merging into existence itself only to become more intensely self-aware than ever. To experience metaconsciousness—direct memory of the interlife—is to reach beyond three-dimensional reality to learn one's reason for being and the nature of personal karmic involvement.*"

Joel Whitton & Joe Fisher
Life Between Life

His book *CE-VI: Close Encounters of a Possession Kind* (1999) introduced ground-breaking concepts and healing modalities for encounters with extraterrestrial entities and dark force entities. His work consolidates traditional shamanism with clinical practices and has helped practitioners discern the difference between spiritual awakenings/experiences and psychosis.

Winifred Lucas (1911–2006), **Hazel Denning** (1920–2008), and **Ron Jue** (1939–2021) co-founded the Association for Past Life Research & Therapies (APRT) in 1981 to be "a clearinghouse for information, set standards and determine ethics, help to articulate the concept of past lives to the professional community, publish a journal, and be involved in a training program. It was also to serve as a support group for its members and as a referral source for the public." In 1986, the purpose of the *Journal of Regression Therapy*, the first journal about regression therapy, was "to include reactions from members, new research, innovative treatment techniques, and personal experiences, as well as articles and book reviews."[86]

APRT transitioned to the International Association for Regression Research and Therapies Inc. (IARRT) in 2014. Even though IARRT no longer exists, archives of the articles in the journal can be found at regressionjournal.org. Other organizations have emerged to continue all aspects of research and excellence in this growing discipline.

The popularity of his books catapulted psychiatrist **Brian Weiss, M.D.** (1944–) beyond his medical practice.

The Cosmology of Reincarnation

Like many of the others, Weiss' unexpected experience with his client was a turning point in his life, a turning point he accepted even though many criticized him. It is undeniable that his books, including *Many Lives, Many Masters: The True Story of a Prominent Psychiatrist, His Young Patient, and the Past-Life Therapy That Changed Both Their Lives* (1988), *Same Soul Many Bodies* (2000), and *Messages from the Masters* (2005), along with his workshops and Past Life Regression trainings have expanded the awareness about past lives worldwide.

Roger Woolger, Ph.D. (1944–2011) made the leap from a rationalistic skeptic trained as a behavioral psychologist at Oxford University to a leader in the field of regression therapy. Disillusioned by his psychology major, he studied comparative religion and Carl Jung's exploration of the personal unconscious and the collective unconscious. A synchronicity when he was asked to review the book *The Cathars and Reincarnation* for the *Journal of the Society for Psychical Research* opened the door for Woolger in 1971, but it was a spontaneous memory of the Cathars eight years later that shifted his perspective about reincarnation. As he reflected on the remembrances, other pieces of his personal history fell into place. Woolger shared his experience and how past life regression therapy evolved his life's work in *Other Lives, Other Selves: A Jungian Psychotherapist Discovers Past Lives* (1988). He created Deep Memory Process® (DMP) which "combines the influences of Jungian active imagination, bodywork from William Reich, psychodrama with shamanic/spirit journeying and integration between lifetimes derived from the Buddhist bardo wisdom of *The Tibetan Book of the Dead*...DMP takes regression therapy out of the narrow confines of hypnotherapy and talk therapy by giving it embodiment and lived experience through psychodrama and bodywork. All levels are worked with the mental, emotional, physical, and spiritual simultaneously."[87]

Shaped by an early eclectic exposure to Hasidism and its roots in the Gerona School and the Kabbalah, Christian Neoplatonism, Tibetan Buddhism, and twentieth century mysticism, **Joel Whitton, M.D., Ph.D.** (1945–2017) approached past life therapy as a forum, an instrument to study the spiritual dimensions of man. Whitton wanted to know what happens after the initial stages of death. In his book, *Life Between Life: Scientific Explorations into the Void Separating One Incarnation from the Next* (1986) with Joe Fisher, Whitton says, "Just as the early psychologists exposed the primitivism of nineteenth-century medicine, contemporary psychological thinking has been similarly revised in the light of more recent evidence. The remarkable healing...has demonstrated that the subconscious is only part of a greater subliminal whole. Past life therapy identifies the higher self that transcends lifetimes and exerts a telling influence on the way we think and behave."[88] Study of the between-life state grew out of Whitton's past life investigations and enhanced knowledge of this higher self. He believed that awareness of the higher self enables people to see their lives from a unique perspective, and awareness of the meaning and purpose of human existence. He describes this heightened awareness as "meta consciousness."

Hasidic Rabbi **Yonasson Gershom** is best known for having written several books on the topic of the Holocaust and reincarnation. *Beyond the Ashes: Cases of Reincarnation from the Holocaust* (1990) and *From Ashes to Healing: Mystical Encounters with the Holocaust* (1996) recounts stories of people who claim to remember the Holocaust. Gershom argues that in the Jewish conception of evil and reincarnation, suffering in this life is not necessarily punishment for wrongdoing in a previous life. He does state that according to the Jewish concept, wickedness can be accumulated over a succession of reincarnations. He cites that Adolf Hitler might have been a reincarnation of the biblical Amalek, a staunch enemy of the Israelites.

As hypnosis and regression therapy evolves, there is a growing interest in Spiritual Hypnosis and Spiritual Regression Therapy. Hypnotherapist, psychologist, psychotherapist, and certified regression therapist **Andy Tomlinson** (1949–) has had a practice since 1996 in the UK. He is the founding director of the International Past Life Regression Academy (established in 2002) to teach others to heal the soul by accessing the true source of emotional challenge and integrating healing through the whole person—physical, emotional, mental, and spiritual. He is the author of *Healing the Eternal Soul* and *Exploring the Eternal Soul* (2006), and the editor of *Transforming the Eternal Soul* (2011). Andy Tomlinson is a founding member of the Spiritual Regression Therapy Association and the Earth

Association of Regression Therapy and has been the President of the Society of Medical Advance and Research with Regression Therapy.

In the past, research about children's past lives focused on validating the children's memories. **Carol Bowman**'s ground-breaking books, *Children's Past Lives: How Past Life Memories Affect Your Child* (1997) and *Return from Heaven: Beloved Relatives Reincarnated Within Your Family* (2001), addressed the subject from a therapeutic point of view. Her story began with her own children, but her research gained footing when more parents reported their children's past life memories. Bowman's books came at a time when reports of children who remembered their past lives were becoming more prevalent in the West, and the Reincarnation Forum on her website gave many an outlet for open discussion long before social media platforms.[89]

Regression therapy took another turn in 1968 when psychologist and Master Hypnotherapist **Michael Newton** (1951–2021) met his client who suffered with depression. When he made the open-ended suggestion to go to the *source* of her pain, she flipped into the afterlife, a period in between her past lives where she met her soul group. Her profound experience of loneliness that had catalyzed her depression was resolved after this reunion. He counted seven thousand clients in his thirty-five years as a hypnotherapist and authored several books about the life between life (LBL) experience including *Destiny of Souls* (2000) and *Journey of Souls* (2010). This expanded the area of study in the field of regression therapy. The Michael

Newton Institute continues Newton's work and offers LBL® training.

Transformation has been a hallmark of **Peter Smith**'s career from the Australian banking industry to his change management consultancy, from his hypnotherapy practice to his work with The Michael Newton Institute, and to the creation of the Quantum Consciousness Experience and the Institute for Quantum Consciousness. The Quantum Consciousness Experience is a spiritual hypnotherapeutic experience that takes the subject through the human portal into ever-expanding realms of consciousness. His book, *Quantum Consciousness: Journey Through Other Realms,* takes the regression experience not only beyond one's current life and the life between lives but also to other worlds.

Management consultant and reincarnation researcher **Hans TenDam** became a pioneer in Regressive Therapy research and practice in the Netherlands. He shares his experiences in his books *Exploring Reincarnation* (2003) and *Deep Healing and Transformation: A Manual of Transpersonal Regression Therapy* (2014). His influence is worldwide as the Founder of TASSO International which organized the World Congresses of Regressive Therapy, and the President of the European Association of Regressive Therapy (EARTH).[90]

While there are skeptics about Past Life Regression Therapy, Eric J. Christopher's research paper "Exploring the Effectiveness of Past-Life Therapy" reveals evidence for Past Life Regression Therapy as a healing modality worthy of exploration. As a holistic approach, Past Life Regression Therapy has demonstrated an individual's profound ability to heal and empower oneself by accessing a higher state of consciousness. In this higher state, the subject can cut through his/her subconscious defense mechanisms and acquire awareness to transcend the blocks.[91]

In his book, *Coming Back: A Psychiatrist Explores Past-Life Journeys,* Raymond Moody, M.D. identified twelve common traits between NDEs and past life regressions. Moody coined the term "near death experience" and has explored this phenomenon for decades.[92] On the other hand, Brian Weiss, M.D., author of several books about past life regression, compares the effect of past life regressions to NDEs. Weiss says "Patients describing their actual deaths in past lives use the same images, accounts, and metaphors as do the children and adults who have had an NDE. The similarities are astounding, even though vivid past-life death descriptions usually come from hypnotized patients with no previous familiarity with the NDE literature. The resemblance of the changes in values, perspective, and outlook on life that typically occur after the experience of an NDE and a past-life recall is also very illuminating. You do not have to be hit by a truck or suffer cardiac arrest to reap increased awareness or spirituality, decline in materialistic worries, the development of a more loving, peaceful nature, or any of the other benefits that past-life regression and near-death experience share."[93]

Christopher says that past life therapists are not as vulnerable to issues about "false memory" as present-life regression therapists. Hans TenDam goes so far as to suggest that many "false memories" are past life images that bleed-over to the present.[94] Roger Woolger says that all memories are mixed with some degree of confabulation.[95] While most therapists do not focus on proving the validity of past life memories, there are several cases where the information gleaned from regression therapy has been proven. Regression therapists focus on helping their clients transcend their presenting problems.

Some researchers focus on measuring the states of consciousness during meditation and hypnosis. Dr. C. Maxwell Cade studied brainwave activity of subjects in various states of consciousness. In a normal waking state of consciousness, people experience EEG brainwave patterns known as Beta which measure at 14 to 22 cycles per second. As one relaxes into a trance-like state, he/she moves into Alpha (8 to 14 cycles per second), Theta (4-8 cycles per second), or Delta (0.5 to 4 cycles per second).[96] Access to one's Higher Self, or the "superconscious" state is achieved while in the Delta state. Research showed it is possible to be in several brainwave levels simultaneously with one level always dominant. Chet Snow and Winifred Lucas also discovered that the therapist as well as the subject showed all four levels of brainwave frequencies.[97]

Today, hypnosis and regression therapy are being widely integrated into all areas of medicine, business, personal development, and spiritual evolution. People from many backgrounds have found a calling as regression therapists. Do they remember other lives as shamans, mesmerists, early hypnotists? If so, have they returned to hone their skills or to function as bodhisattvas to aid the evolution of humanity?

4 MY COSMOLOGY

Even though I am not a scholar, I had always sensed the Universe orchestrating events in my life, dangling "spiritual carrots" in front of me encouraging me to push on. My father was Buddhist but that was not where I began my research after his spirit came to me, showed me his afterlife, and inspired me to learn more about reincarnation. Instead, a miraculous event occurred that guided me to Dr. Brian Weiss's book *Many Lives, Many Masters: The True Story of a Prominent Psychiatrist, His Young Patient, and the Past Life Therapy that Changed Both Their Lives*. Next, conversations with Dad's spirit showed me his Buddhist beliefs and conversations with my brother-in-law exposed me to Rudolph Steiner and Anthroposophy. Conversations with my son-in-law and his Druze family showed me yet another point of view. I know it was no coincidence meeting Weiss, Roger Woolger, Patricia Walsh, Carol Bowman, Janet Cunningham, Ruth Montgomery, Christopher Bache, Walter Semkiw, Jim Tucker, Antonia Mills, James Matlock, Peter Smith, and Rabih Elawar. More carrots teased me forward, but reading and hearing about reincarnating is one thing while experiencing memories and reliving other lives is quite different. I searched for signs of a theory of the cosmology of reincarnation in the notes about my personal memories of multiple lifetimes, interlife experiences, and Oneness. After studying reincarnation research and regression therapy for over thirty years, I wondered if there was a theory that unified all traditions and therapy practices.

Before I share MY theory, I want to say that it is an evolving process and that it might be different from yours or anyone else's. In fact, *honoring many theories that are evolving is the first premise of MY cosmology*. In addition, my theory is based on mystical experiences that happened spontaneously and/or during meditation as well as during a regression.

Let me begin with **Oneness/Source/All That Is/Tao**—the state of being one with the Universe. Although my experiences with Source are ineffable, the feeling of "unconditional love" was far beyond any concept of love I have ever known. I saw what I call a "shadowless light" that is both brilliant and gentle. You hear stories about the "White Light," but I knew this light was all-encompassing and cast no shadow. I sensed "unity consciousness" with all beings—a feeling of "no separation."

In this energy of unconditional love, pure light, and unity consciousness, I felt an *urge* to create beauty and harmony, and then I sensed the moment **I individuated out of Oneness creating an Oversoul**. It was my "big bang" moment. It was a glorious moment. My Oversoul began the process of incarnating. *Each incarnation is connected to the Oversoul and to one another via a stream of consciousness and yet each retains autonomy over itself.*

I chose a variety of experiences because I could. Like an actor, director, and writer of my own series, I explored the "what ifs." Because Earth is a dualistic environment, I began to accumulate energies, both positive and negative. This will continue until I master these energies and learn how to navigate them, just as we learned to fly airplanes after we harnessed the natural laws of gravity.

In my cosmology, incarnation in the **Earth Experience** is an honor. **It is a choice to experience free will.** It is an opportunity to experience the **physical world, sensations, and emotions**. It is also an opportunity to experience the **non-physical world**, both the between-lives realms and the realms where consciousness goes during dreams or altered states. They are two aspects of the Earth experience. Most people focus on the physical world, but the non-physical world is equally important. Just as the stratosphere surrounds Earth, and all the planets and stars fill a small percentage of the sky, matter is a small portion of the Universe. They are interconnected. So too are the physical and non-physical worlds, each governed by laws of nature.

Before each incarnation, we create a **purpose**, a mission. *Our common mission is to be an expression of the energy of*

Source in the Earth experience, to embody Divine Love in the physical world. In fact, it is our destiny—yet we also possess the free will to choose when and how we do so.

Navigating duality is an aspect of the Earth experience and transcending duality is another. It is an **AND/ALSO** concept just as Newtonian and Quantum physics operate simultaneously.

Unconditional love is our true nature and the fulcrum of every experience. The pendulum of experiences will swing back and forth until it rests in the center, which is Divine Love, union with Source. Although our spiritual nature appears to be the opposite of our material nature and we oscillate between them, we desire balance between both. As individuated aspects of Source, love and compassion are encoded within us.

Our imbalances are lessons about love. The lower vibrations of self may perceive these experiences from an egoic point of view and the knee-jerk reaction of retribution, an eye for an eye. The Soul's point of view acknowledges the lesson for growth, acts accordingly, and seeks the answer within the self for the outward imbalance. As one achieves balance, one can attract other lessons via joy and creativity.

Collectively, we have a way to go, but individually we are free to choose our way. As more individuals choose to align with Source, momentum grows for the collective until it reaches "critical mass," a turning point in the evolution of humankind. In the history of the human species, there have been such points—the rise of consciousness about organic food, about the definition of marital unions, about women's rights, rights of the people vs. a monarchy, and about freedom of religion. These shifts in collective consciousness are still a work in progress.

As an individual, you can reflect on how the issues of the collective consciousness connect with you and you can act on a personal level to do something for the greater good of the collective. As an individual within a community, you can commune with others for the greater good. Your challenges and successes indicate where you are in your evolutionary process.

Just as there are **stages** of life in the physical world—birth, childhood, adolescence, adulthood, elderhood, and death—there are also stages in the non-physical world. There is a welcoming stage, a processing stage, a debriefing stage, a reintegration stage, and a planning stage for the next incarnation. The experiences in the stages of the non-physical world reflect one's evolutionary process.

There are **helpers in both worlds who guide, heal, educate**, and **hold the energy of love**. The guides sense when a person is ready to move into another stage. They create clever ways/glitches/anomalies for a person to discover for themselves that there is more and guide them compassionately to the next level.

There is **no judgment** about the experiences one

chooses, although **accountability for one's actions carries over from the physical world to the nonphysical world, and back again**. Actions not aligned with the energy of Source will eventually seek balance, but there is no judgment about how long or the number of incarnations it takes.

I see the natural **laws of karma** as a system that governs the evolution of humankind. It is a compassionate system of accountability where our actions—including our thoughts and words—have an energy aligned with our Higher Self or not. There is a kind of **spiritual ledger** where negative actions create debits to one's account and positive actions create credits. Actions not aligned with one's Higher Self create opportunities to gain experience about where one is separated from Self/Source/Love. They create a debit in the ledger, also known as negative karma. Repeated negative actions generate interest on the debt and therefore bigger lessons. Course corrections balance out charges. Actions aligned with one's Higher Self create a credit to the ledger, or positive karma. Repeated positive actions create bonus points and opportunities to manifest one's purpose.

We choose the Earth experience not just for the experience but also for a **higher purpose**. There are two higher purposes. **The first is to integrate our True Essence—that which emanates from Source—with**

The Cosmology of Reincarnation

our physical body, sensations, and experiences. **The second is to share experiences with everyone and everything through relationships with others, with all creatures, and with the world. How we choose to express our True Essence is up to us.**

Reincarnation is **an open-ended system that evolves as we do**, and I recognize that we have evolved beyond traditional beliefs about reincarnation. The way to grasp this evolution is to **expand our consciousness** just as the James Webb Space Telescope flew further out into our Universe and gave us clearer pictures of it than we have seen before.

I also sense that by understanding the system I would have a handle on how to collaborate with it as part of the healing and co-creating process. Just as we used the laws of physics to fly an airplane, we can transcend "constructs" we have subconsciously built that have held us back from our True Essence. The key to this transformation is being consciously aware. It is the first step of the process and there are many steps. Once you become conscious, you cannot "unring the bell." The more consciously aware you are, the more you attract experiences to further your evolution.

Each incarnated Soul carries a **collection of imprints of aspects** orchestrated by one's Oversoul, lessons designed to develop the Soul's ability to manifest his/her Purpose. Multiple incarnates may carry like energies—entangled shared aspects—but **each Soul is only responsible for his/her own actions**.

My studies have shown **patterns in the reincarnation process** including:

1. forgetting/veil of separation
2. themes repeated in multiple lives with variations on the theme
3. bonding—both positively and negatively—drawing people together in love and hate
4. triggers that stir one's memories
5. balancing of energies through the law of karma
6. a progressive build-up of energy that once it is recognized and corrected, progressively decreases until it becomes a "non-issue"
7. a sort of grace that manifests when one awakens to the above.

A **veil of separation** exists between entities and the Oversoul like the veil between consciousness and subconsciousness. As an entity remembers his/her connection to Source, the veil becomes thinner. Communication between other lives and Source occurs. When an entity awakens to the consequences of his/her actions and makes course corrections, he/she has a quantum effect on the entangled shared aspects. This quantum effect ripples through each entity's lineage, and beyond all timelines to all entities who share aspect themes. Just as technology is speeding up everything in the material world, *the quantum effect is expanding the collective consciousness into new frontiers.*

When we remember these things, we know that *everyone is also on their path*, and we can hold them in the energy of unconditional love and compassion.

Before we incarnate, we choose topics—**themes**—to experience, and these repeat throughout our life with variations on the theme. When the lessons about the topic are not learned, they will repeat in other lives with more variations including experiencing the opposite sides. Just as our school lessons become more complex as we advance in knowledge and ability, multiple themes entangled together can challenge us to evolve.

We can develop relationships with "**soul groups**" in the non-physical world and decide to experience incarnating together. When we reunite with someone from our soul group, we feel a connection. Sometimes, we agree to play adversarial/antagonistic roles with our soul group members. These bonds—whether positive or negative—draw us together, but in the physical world the veil of forgetfulness prevents us from seeing the non-physical intention behind our relationships. The blockage to full understanding challenges us to remember and can trigger us to seek answers. How we interact with others creates a chain reaction—a "karmic snowball" of energy that builds until we address it. The snowball begins to melt when we make progress with a lesson until it melts completely.

Besides reunions with soul group members, other things or events can **"trigger"** memories of other lives. A smell, a sound, touching something, seeing an object, seeing a movie, or reading a book about a particular topic can trigger an emotional or visceral response. Déjà vu could be a glimpse or preview of past life memories bubbling up to the surface.

The laws of karma work differently in the physical world versus the non-physical world. One can experience an awakening in either world; however, there are limitations in the non-physical world. When one has an awakening and realizes the consequences of one's actions in the non-physical world, one can simulate the concept of course corrections, but until one conducts those actions in the physical world, they are "thought exercises." Through altered states of consciousness in either world, one can practice the right actions until they become imprinted. As previously mentioned, there are helpers to guide one through the process and to hold the energy of unconditional love. They do so with compassion rather than judgment. The process is about understanding one's own actions or reactions. It is not about revenge or retribution. When one heals an unresolved issue completely, it becomes a "non-issue" regardless of whether the other person participates in the resolution or not.

If the other person does not participate in the resolution, he/she will attract a substitute person—a **surrogate**—to work out the issue. Surrogates who share similar lessons can also come into our lives to help us work on an issue when the actual soul who was involved with us is not available, just as a spouse can reflect an unresolved issue with one's parent.

It is both our free will choice and destiny to balance our positive and negative karma to embody unconditional love and creativity in the physical world. *How we express unconditional love and creativity is our gift to the Universe.*

Each of us will assess our actions and make course corrections until we are in harmony with Source. There are infinite opportunities to do so. The assessment in the non-physical world is called a "life review," but it can also occur in the physical world. For instance, one could have a midlife crisis that makes one question everything. People experienced this effect during the pandemic. In the Twelve Steps program, one is guided to do a review of how one's actions have harmed others. During a powerful moment in the Life Between Life process, one goes to the life review of the life revisited and witnesses how one's actions affected others.

The Cosmology of Reincarnation

Our guides watch over us and orchestrate or oversee experiences to help us remember our Purpose. This can come in the form of nudging us toward a book at just the right moment or pointing us in a direction that serendipitously turns out to be synchronistic to something we were thinking about. And as we pay attention to the nudges and synchronicities—as we observe our reactions to the triggers, and even bring our awareness to memories of other lives—we open ourselves to **grace** or **divine intervention**. Miraculous events happen that are beyond explanation.

These processes happen over what we perceive to be time, which itself is subjective. Measuring time in the physical world is not an exact science and has been a challenge throughout the ages. The lunar month is not 28 days but 28.3 days. The solar year (365.2425 days as defined in the Gregorian calendar) has to be adjusted with leap years and leap seconds. Time in the physical world is a "mental construct," but it is one of several mental constructs in the non-physical world. Some who cross over from the physical world to the non-physical world do not understand where they are, so they create mental constructs depending on their beliefs of a time they prefer, or they repeat their death circumstances in a continuous loop. When they awaken to what has happened, guides greet them and usher them to the appropriate place, with "place" being a particular experience of consciousness. For instance, one might go to a place of healing—a place where one can rest and relax—or go to places of learning where there is the opportunity to review the previous life and plan one's next incarnation. Each of these places is designed to nurture and support souls on their spiritual journey. I described my experiences of all the phases in my book *Unstuck in Time*.

The system of reincarnation is mind-blowing when you consider all the above. It makes our current technology (closed circuit television, algorithms, and AI) look primitive by comparison. I will admit that it feels a bit like *The Matrix*. Although I have penetrated through many veils of separation, I admit that there is more I know I do not know—at least, not yet. However, by observing how it works, I have learned to collaborate with it to clear old karma wherever it originated, even across multiple timelines. I feel as if I have picked weeds out of my garden before renourishing it for a new crop (my life purpose). I have been able to grow/manifest things I had not dreamed possible. Indeed, now beginning to grasp my potential in this process of soul evolution, I feel the urge to master the energies of Earth's Garden to create even more, albeit in other lifetimes.

Meditation and regression therapy have expanded my conscious awareness not only across timelines to the past but also to the future, including future events in this life that I then experienced. These practices have helped me come back to the center of my being, to unconditional love/Source. Even though I feel so new to this way of thinking, I look forward to developing my skills to become more adept at the Earth experience to fully embody my True Essence in the material world.

Remember what I said at the beginning of this chapter. This is an evolving process. Who knows what we are becoming as we evolve? Will we become a new species? Will we discover we are descendants from or progenitors of other worlds or that we are all avatars in a video game or simulation? And what will become of those who do not choose to evolve—to expand their consciousness? Will they become extinct like Neanderthal?

As I contemplate what I have experienced so far and the infinite possibilities, I feel an urge pulling me to the "edge of infinity." I can hardly wait to discover what awaits me there. Until then, I intend to live each moment as best I can and to be an expression of unconditional love.

I hope *The Cosmology of Reincarnation and Rebirth* has helped you understand the reincarnation process. I hope it will inspire your memories of Source, unconditional love, and your mission on Earth.

GLOSSARY

Akh – Egyptian: the spark of God.
Alternate realities – a synonym for a parallel universe.
al-Wahm al-Amil – Persian: hypnosis.
American Esotericism – the occult and mystical interpretations of America's past that dominates the National Redemption Party and serves as the de facto religion of America.
Anatman – Sanskrit: "no soul."
Anatta – Pali: "no soul."
ancestral worship – contact with the spirits of departed family/clan.
animal magnetism – a force/power in the bodies of animals, including humans.
Animism – the belief in a vital life force of all natural things (plants, animals, earth, elements) including the belief in personal souls.
Anthroposophy – from Greek: *anthropo*/human and *sophia*/wisdom. Founded in the early 20th century by the Rudolf Steiner.
Arhats – Buddhism and Jainism: someone who has attained the goal of the religious life .
artificial somnambulism – an abnormal condition of sleep-in which motor acts (such as walking) are performed.
aspect/fragment – a particular status or phase in which something appears.

Ba – Egyptian: the eternal soul.
Bardo – the intermediate or astral state of the soul after death and before rebirth.
berdaches – hermaphrodites (Indigenous cultures).
Bodhisattvas – a being that compassionately refrains from entering nirvana to save others and is worshipped as a deity in Mahayana Buddhism.
Brahmins – a Hindu of the highest caste traditionally assigned to the priesthood.
Buddha – Sanskrit: "enlightened"; akin to Sanskrit "bodhi" for enlightenment.
Camaquen – Incan: the spirit of dead.
Cathars – a member of one of various ascetic and dualistic Christian sects, especially of the later Middle Ages, teaching that matter is evil and professing faith in an angelic Christ who did not really undergo human birth or death.
channeler – a person who conveys thoughts or energy from a source believed to be outside the person's body or conscious mind.
collective karma – the belief that the karma of a nation, organization, association, or group accumulates because of the collective actions and decisions.
concurrent reincarnation – the belief that more than one spirit may occupy a single body simultaneously.
CORT – cases of the reincarnation type, as designated by the Dept. of Perceptual Studies at the University of Virginia

CORT-1 – cases of the reincarnation type with memories of the intermission between incarnations, as designated by the Dept. of Perceptual Studies at the University of Virginia.

cult of the dead – Druid: ritualistic beheading because the soul was thought to reside in the head.

Devachan – Hinduism, Theosophy: the dwelling place of the gods.

Dharma – your life purpose, the path of righteousness.

Dispositional karma – the belief that an internal psychological law manifested in thoughts, feelings, and behavior.

DMP – Deep Memory Process created by Roger Woolger, a regression technique which combines the influences of Jungian active imagination, body work from William Reich, psychodrama with shamanic/spirit journeying, and integration between lifetimes derived from the Buddhist bardo wisdom of *The Tibetan Book of the Dead*.

Dream temples – Egyptian: temples dedicated to sleep/dream.

Druze – a branch that emerged in Egypt as an off-shoot or subset of Islam in 1017; found in Lebanon, Syria, Jordan, Israel, and as immigrants in other countries.

EEG – electroencephalogram.

Ego strengthening statements – a form of autosuggestion created by Emile Coue.

Elysium – the home of the blessed after death in Greek and Roman mythology.

Emin – Nigeria: spiritual body, which is the seat of life for the Yoruba people.

etheric double – subtle energy body.

Gilgulum –Jewish: term for "the revolving of souls through a succession of lives." It goes back to the time of Moses.

Gita – "Bhagavad Gita" (Sanskrit: "The Beautiful Song by God"), a 700-verse Hindu scripture dated to the first millennium BCE and considered to be one of the holy scriptures for Hinduism.

Gnosticism – the thought and practice especially of various cults of late pre-Christian and early Christian centuries distinguished by the conviction that matter is evil, and that emancipation comes through gnosis.

Hades – the land of the dead in Greek mythology ruled by the Greek god of the underworld.

Haplogroups – a group of similar haplotypes that share a common ancestor with a single-nucleotide polymorphism mutation.

Haplotypes – group of alleles in an organism that are inherited together from a single parent.

Harvest – graduation into the density/vibrations most comfortable to them, according to the Law of One teachings.

Hasidism– mystical movement that originated among Eastern European Jews in the 18th century and includes belief in reincarnation.

Hermaphrodites – in biology, an organism with both reproductive organs (male/female).

Humanism Movement – a philosophical stance that emphasizes the individual and social potential, and agency of human beings, whom it considers the starting point for serious moral and philosophical inquiry.

Hypnosis – a trancelike state that resembles sleep but is induced by a person whose suggestions are readily accepted by the subject.

Hypnotherapy – a therapeutic technique that uses hypnosis to shift the subject's state of consciousness to allow focused concentration.

hypnotism – word coined by Etienne Felix d'Henin de Cuviller in 1826 from neuro-hypnotism (nervous sleep).

Inquisition – an institution within the Catholic Church whose aim was to combat heresy, conducting trials of suspected heretics.

intermission memories – memories of the experience between incarnations.

Inua u'we –Aboh (Nigeria): "returning to life."

Jainism – a religion of India originating in the sixth century BCE and teaching liberation of the soul by right knowledge, right faith, and right conduct.

Juridical karma – the belief that the way we conduct ourselves in one life affects us in that life or another one.

Ka – Egyptian: spirit/lower energy that is not eternal and needs to be activated.

Kabbalah – Hebrew: reception, tradition, or correspondence; an esoteric method, discipline, and school of thought in Jewish mysticism (third century BCE).

karet – Jewish: "cut off."
karma – Sanskrit: concept of action, work or deed, and its effect or consequences.
Khat – Egyptian: the physical element of being.
kilpot – Jewish: "negative shells."
Kriyamana karma – a type of karma whose consequences are experienced in this very life.
Kuci – a Nupe (Nigeria) term meaning "personal soul" which is said to animate the child of descendants at birth.
LBL – Life Between Life experience.
Lethe – the River of Forgetfulness (Greek mythology).
Levant – a large area in the Eastern Mediterranean region of Western Asia.
life review – a review of one's previous life during the intermission period between incarnations.
Lord Maitreya (Sanskrit) – regarded as the future Buddha of this world in Buddhist eschatology.
Lun Hue – a Taoist term meaning "return cycle" (Lun/wheel or cycle, Hue/return.
Mahayana Buddhism – "Great Vehicle": term for a broad group of Buddhist traditions, texts, philosophies, and practices. Mahayana Buddhism developed in ancient India (c. 1st century BCE onwards) and is considered one of the three main existing branches of Buddhism (the other being Theravada and Vajrayana).
major cycle – harvests which occur after each twenty-five-thousand-year cycle, according to the Law of One.

master cycle – harvests which occur after the seventy-five-thousand-year cycle, according to the Law of One.
Mesmerism – a force/power in the bodies of animals, including humans (concept from Franz Anton Mesmer).
Meta Consciousness – a heightened awareness of the higher self where the percipient loses all sense of personal identity by merging into existence itself to become more intensely self-aware (coined by Joel Whitton).
Metempsychosis – the process where the mind transmigrates; a unit of consciousness (our divine identity) takes a different form to experience a variety of characteristics within the field of creation.
Metensomatosis – the passage of the immortal soul from one human body to another after a period in the Otherworld.
mitzvah of Yabim – a Jewish term meaning "the obligation of the brother of a childless."
mitzvot – a Jewish term meaning "an obligation."
Monad – the concept of "one essence" in the metaphysical and theological theory; the most primal aspect of God in Gnosticism.
MRI – Magnetic Resonance Imaging.
multiple simultaneous reincarnation – belief where a spirit occupies more than one body at the same time, also called soul splitting or split souls.
Multiverses – a hypothetical group of multiple universes. Together, these universes are presumed to comprise everything that exists: the entirety of space, time, matter, energy, information, and the physical laws and

constants that describe them.
Myth of Er – a myth in *The Republic* by Socrates.
Nāṭiq – the name for a male who remembers and talks about a previous live(s) in the Druze culture.
Nāṭiqa – the name for a female who remembers and talks about a previous life or lives in the Druze culture.
NDE – Near-Death Experience where a person dies for a brief period but returns to life again.
Nkrabea – an Akan (Ghana) term meaning "individual essence or destiny" conferred by Nyankopan, an aspect of God.
Nuṭq – the phenomena of remembering and talking about a previous life or lives in the Druze culture.
Nyankopan – an Akan (Ghana) term meaning "an aspect of God."
Okan – a Yoruba (Nigeria) term meaning "heart soul."
oracle bones – (Chinese:) – pieces of ox scapula and turtle plastron, which were used for pyromancy a form of divination in ancient China, mainly during the late Shang dynasty.
Ouija board – also known as a spirit board or talking board – a flat board marked with the letters of the Latin alphabet, the numbers 0–9, the words "yes", "no", occasionally "hello" and "goodbye", along with various symbols and graphics. It uses a planchette (small heart-shaped piece of wood or plastic) as a movable indicator to spell out messages during a séance.
parallel lives – parallel events or situations happen at the same time as one another, or are similar to one another.

past life regression – a therapeutic technique for accessing and re-experiencing your past lives directly.

Past Life Regression Therapy – a therapeutic technique that uses hypnosis and guided meditation, often in combination with other healing modalities such as Reiki and EFT (Emotional Freedom Technique), to recall past lives.

PET – Positron Emission Tomography – a functional imaging technique that uses radioactive substances known as radiotracers to visualize and measure changes in metabolic processes, and in other physiological activities including blood flow, regional chemical composition, and absorption.

prarabdha karma – that part of your sanchita karma currently activated in your present life, and which influences the course of your present life.

processional karma – operates within an individual's mind or psyche. It may involve self-judgment, but it originates from an internal force rather than an external one (coined by James Matlock).

Punabbhava – Buddhist term meaning "again existence."

QCE – Quantum Consciousness Experience, created by Peter Smith.

QHHT – a form of hypnosis created by Dolores Cannon that enables direct communication with the subconscious for answers to any question.

rebirth – a belief that a part of a being survives physical death to be reborn in a new body.

Reformation Movement – a major movement within Western Christianity in 16th-century Europe that posed a religious and political challenge to the Catholic Church and in particular to papal authority, arising from what were perceived to be errors, abuses, and discrepancies by the Catholic Church.

Regression therapy – is a therapy that focuses on any past memory, such as past events of the current life or of previous lives.

reincarnation – to be made flesh again, the belief that a part of a being survives physical death, to be reborn in a new body.

replacement reincarnation – the belief that a spirit replaces the original spirit without the body dying.

retributive karma – the belief that direct justice manifests physically, i.e., an eye for an eye.

samskaras – Hinduism: dispositional karmic traits.

sanchita karma – the sum of the accumulated karma of previous lives.

sleep temples – Egyptian: temples dedicated to sleep/dream.

somnambulism – abnormal condition of sleeping in which motor acts (such as walking) are performed.

soul matrix – the idea that the soul is bound in an energy that links the past, present, or future (coined by Dick Sutphen).

Spirit Releasement Therapy (SRT) – a therapeutic technique to release spirit attachments, especially dark energies. It is a form of shadow work where light overcomes darkness.

split souls – parallel lives of the same soul, but with the contract to meet, interact, learn lessons, or have a mission together.

Sufism – a mystical branch of Islam that emerged early on in Islamic history partly as a reaction again the worldliness of the early Umayyad Ciphate (seventh century C.E.).

superconscious mind – often referred to as the higher Self, a state above subconsciousness and consciousness, connecting you to a higher state of being and functioning.

Tao – aka Dao – the natural order of the universe, whose character one's intuition must discern to realize the potential for individual wisdom, as conceived in the context of East Asian philosophy, East Asian religions, or any other philosophy or religion that aligns to this principle.

The Republic – Greek: a Socratic dialogue, authored by Plato around 375 BCE, concerning justice, the order and character of the just city-state, and the just man. It is Plato's best-known work, and one of the world's most influential works of philosophy and political theory.

Theosophical Society – an organization established in the United States during the late 19th century, founded primarily by the Russian Helena Blavatsky, drawing its teachings predominantly from Blavatsky's writings.

Theosophy – categorized by scholars of religion as both a new religious movement and as part of the occultist stream of Western esotericism, it draws upon both older European philosophies such as Neoplatonism and Asian religions such as Hinduism and Buddhism.

Theravada Buddhism – literally "The Way of the Elders" or the "School of the Elders," the most commonly accepted name of Buddhism's oldest existing school.

Tirthankaras – progenitor/supreme preachers of Dharma (Jains).

Transcendentalism – one of the first philosophical, spiritual, and literary movements that developed in the New England area of the US in the early 19th century. It developed as a reaction to intellectualism and spirituality of the time. Its core belief is in the inherent goodness of people and nature, in the divinity in everyday experience, and in the dynamic processes of physical and spiritual phenomena.

Transmigration – "Trans" means beyond, and "migration" means change of residence. The migration of the soul to a different body after death, or to go from one state of existence or place to another. There are two types of transmigration: metempsychosis and metensomatosis. Metempsychosis refers to the transmigration at death of the soul of a human being or animal into a new body of the same or a distinct species. Metensomatosis, on the other hand, refers to the passage of the immortal soul from one human body to another after a period in the Otherworld.

Upanishads – Sanskrit: late Vedic texts that supplied the basis of later Hindu philosophy, the most recent part of the Vedas, the oldest scriptures of Hinduism. They deal with meditation, philosophy, consciousness, and ontological knowledge as well as mantras, benedictions, rituals, ceremonies, and sacrifices.

Vedas – Sanskrit: "knowledge," "vision," or "wisdom." The oldest scriptures of Hinduism (1500-1200 BCE).
Xibalba – Incan: afterlife.

REFERENCE LIST

Books
100 Cases of Reincarnation Among the Dong People, a study of the Dong tribes of China, Changzhen Li, independently published, 2020
Adventures in Consciousness, Jane Roberts, Bantam Doubleday Dell, 1985
American Rebirth: Reincarnation Belief Among North American Indians and Inuit, Antonia Mills and Richard Slobodin, University of Toronto Press; 2nd ed. Edition, 1994
Autobiography of a Yogi, Paramahansa Yogananda, Sterling Publishers Pvt. Ltd; UK ed. edition, 2020
Beyond the Ashes, Rabbi Yonasson Gershom, Are Press; First Edition, 1992
Children who speak of past-life experiences: Is there a psychological explanation? Erlendur Haraldsson Psychology and Psychotherapy,
Research and Practice (2003) 76, 55-57 (The British Psychological Society)
Children's Past Lives: How Past Life Memories Affect Your Child, Carol Bowman, Bantam, 1998
China: A History (Volume 1): From Neolithic Cultures through the Great Qing Empire, (10,000 BCE - 1799 CE), Harold M. Tanner, Hackett Publishing Co. Inc., 2010
Destiny of Souls, Michael Newton, Llewellyn Publications; Subsequent edition, 2010

Earth Energies: A Quest for the Hidden Power of the Planet, Serge Kahili King, Quest Books; First Edition, 1992

Exploring Reincarnation: The Classic Guide to the Evidence for Past-Life Experiences, Hans TenDam, Random House UK, 2003

Exploring the Eternal Soul, Andy Tomlinson, From the Heart Press; 2nd New Section Added Edition, 2012

Findings in Hypnosis, Dave Elman, Dave Elman; First Edition, 1964

Five Lives Remembered, Dolores Cannon, Ozark Mountain Publishing; Illustrated edition, 2009

From Ashes to Healing: Mystical Encounters with the Holocaust, Rabbi Yonasson Gershom, ARE Press, 1996

Harper's Encyclopaedia of Mystical and Paranormal Experience, Rosemary Ellen Guiley, Harper San Francisco; First Edition, 1991

Healing in Hypnosis, Milton Erickson, Irvington Publishers, 1983 (available on archive.org)

Healing the Eternal Soul: Insights from Past Life and Spiritual Regression, Andy Tomlinson, From the Heart Press; 2nd edition, 2012

I Saw the Light and Came Here: Children's Experience of Reincarnation, Erlendur Haraldsson and James Matlock, White Crow Books, 2017

Isis Unveiled, H.P. Blavatsky, theosophicalsociety.org, 1877

Journey of Souls: Case Studies of Life Between Lives, Michael Newton, Llewellyn Publications; First Edition, 1994

Life Before Life: Is There Life Before Birth? 750 Cases of Hyp-

nosis, Helen Wambach, White Crow Books, 2020

Life Between Life: Scientific Explorations into the Void Separating One Incarnation from the Next, Joel Whitton and Joe Fisher, Dolphin; First Edition, 1986

Lifecycles: Reincarnation and the Web of Life, Christopher Bache, Paragon House; Reprint edition, 1998

Life Reframing in Hypnosis, Milton Erickson, Irvington Pub; First Edition, 1984

Living with Joy: Keys to Personal Power and Spiritual Transformation (Earth Life Series, 1), Sanaya Roman, HJ Kramer/New World Library; 25th Anniversary edition, 2011

LSD and the Mind of the Universe: Diamond from Heaven, Christopher Bache, Park Street Press, 2019

Magick in Theory and Practice, Aleister Crowley, publisher not identified, 1929 (available on archive.org)

Many Lives Many Masters: The True Story of a Prominent Psychiatrist, His Young Patient, and the Past-Life Therapy that Changed Both Their Lives, Brian Weiss, Fireside, 1988

Messages from the Masters, Brian Weiss, Balance; Warner Books, Reprint edition, 2008

Mind-Body Communication in Hypnosis (The Seminars, Workshops, and Lectures of Milton H. Erickson, Vol. 3), Milton Erickson, Irvington Pub; First Edition, 1987

Oldest Books in the World, Isaac Myer, Research Associates School Times Publications & Frontline Distribution International Inc., 2010

Other Lives, Other Selves: A Jungian Psychotherapist Discovers Past Lives, Roger Woolger, Random House Publishing

Group; Reissue edition, 1988
Exploring Reincarnation, Hans TenDam, Lulu.com, 2012
Past Lives, Future Loves, Dick Sutphen, Pocket, 1987
Personal Power through Awareness: A Guidebook for Sensitive People (Book II of the Earth Life Series), Sanaya Roman, HJ Kramer, 1986
Quantum Consciousness: Journey through other Realms, Peter Smith, Llewellyn Publications; Illustrated edition, 2018
Reincarnation and Biology: A Contribution to the Etiology of Birthmarks and Birth Defects, Ian Stevenson, Praeger, 1997
Reincarnation and Karma: Two Fundamental Truths of Human Existence, Rudolph Steiner, SteinerBooks, 2001
Reincarnation Beliefs of North American Indians, Warren Jefferson, Native Voices; First Edition, 2009
Reincarnation: The Phoenix Fire Mystery, Joseph Head and S.L. Cranston, Julian Press/Crown; 5th Printing edition, 1977
Reliving Past Lives: The Evidence Under Hypnosis, Helen Wambach, Barnes & Noble Books; Second Printing edition, 2000
Return from Heaven: Beloved Relatives Reincarnated Within Your Family, Carol Bowman, Harper; 1st edition, 2001
Same Soul Many Bodies: Discover the Healing Power of Future Lives through Progression Therapy, Brian Weiss, Free Press; Later Printing edition, 2005
Seth Material, Jane Roberts, New Awareness Network; 1st edition, 2010
Shamanism: Archaic Techniques of Ecstasy, Mircea Iliade,

The Cosmology of Reincarnation
Princeton University Press, 1964
Signs of Reincarnation: Exploring Beliefs, Cases, and Theory, James Matlock, Rowman & Littlefield Publishers, 2019
Spiritual Growth: Being your Higher Self, Sanaya Roman, HJ Kramer; 1st edition, 1992
The Akan Doctrine of God: A Fragment of Gold Coast Ethics and Religion, Joseph B. Danquah, Routledge; 1st edition, 2017
The Case of Reincarnation, Joe Fisher, Bantam, 1985
The Cathars and Reincarnation, Arthur Guirdham and C.W. Daniel; Reprint edition, 2004
The Convoluted Universe (five volumes), Dolores Cannon, Ozark Mountain Publishing, 2015
The Historie of Travaile into Virginia Britannia, William Strachey, Printed for the Hakluyt Society, 1849 (available on archive.org)
The Nature of Personal Reality: Specific Practical Techniques for Solving Everyday Problems and Enriching the Life You Know, Jane Roberts, Amber-Allen Publ., New World Library; Reprint edition, 1994
The Power Within, Alexander Cannon, Dutton, 1953
The Secret Doctrine, H.P. Blavatsky, Theosophical University Press, 1888
The Three Waves of Volunteers and the New Earth, Dolores Cannon, Ozark Mountain Publishing, 2011
The Tibetan Book of the Dead: First Complete Translation, Graham Coleman (Editor), Thupten Jinpa (Editor), Gyurme Dorje (Translator), Penguin Classics; Deluxe edition, 2007

The Unquiet Dead: A Psychologic Treats Spirit Possession, Edith Fiore, Ballantine Books, 1995

Thirty Years Among the Dead, Carl Wickland, White Crow Books, 2011 (available on archive.org)

Transforming the Eternal Soul: Further Insights from Regression Therapy, Andy Tomlinson, From The Heart Press, 2011

Twenty Cases Suggestive of Reincarnation, Cases of the Reincarnation Type, Ian Stevenson, University of Virginia Press; Revised and Enlarged edition, 1980

Two Hundred Queries Moderately Propounded Concerning the Doctrine of Humane Souls, and Its Conformity to the Truths of Christianity, Franciscus Mercurius van Helmont, EEBO Editions, ProQuest, 2011

Visbuddhi Margo (Path of Purity), Buddhghosha, London Published for the Pali Text Society by Oxford University Press, 1922 (available on archive.org)

You have Been Here Before: A Psychologist Looks at Past Lives, Edith Fiore, National Guild of Hypnotists, Inc., 2005

You Were Born Again to be Together, Dick Sutphen, Pocket; First Edition, 1976

Zohar, the Book of Splendor, Schocken, 1995

Articles and Papers

Development of Certainty About the Correct Deceased Person in a Case of the Reincarnation Type in Lebanon: The Case of Nasih Al-Danaf, Erlendur Haraldsson and Majd Abu-Izzeddin, Journal of Scientific Exploration, Vol. 16, No. 3, 2002 https://www.scientificexploration.org/docs/16/jse_16_3_haraldsson.pdf

Exploring the Effectiveness of Past-Life Therapy, Eric J. Christopher, A Research Paper submitted in partial fulfillment of the requirements for a Master of Science degree, University of Wisconsin-Stout, 2000

Persistence of "Past-Life" Memories in Adults Who, in their Childhood, and

Claimed Memories of a Past Life, Erlendur Haraldsson and Majd Abu-Izzeddin, The Journal of Nervous and Mental Disease, Vol. 200, No. 11, 2012

https://journals.lww.com/jonmd/abstract/2012/11000/persistence_of__past_life__memories_in_adults_who,.13.asp

Videos and Links

13000-year-old beer, https://www.smithsonianmag.com/smart-news/traces-13000-year-old-beer-found-israel-180970282/

Abbe Faria, https://en.wikipedia.org/wiki/Abb%C3%A9_Faria

African Reincarnation Beliefs, Andrew Rook, Reincarnation in African Traditional Religion (theosophy-nw.org)

Answering Your Questions about Reincarnation with Gil Shir–Kabbalah Explained Simply–YouTube
https://www.youtube.com/watch?v=AQHTjQjoeQo

A Secret of Reincarnation, Michael Berg
https://kabbalah.com/en/articles/secret-reincarnation/

Ambroise-Auguste Liebeault,

https://en.wikipedia.org/wiki/Ambroise-Auguste_Li%C3%A9beault
Anatta, https://en.wikipedia.org/wiki/Anatta
Ancient Egyptian afterlife beliefs, https://en.wikipedia.org/wiki/Ancient_Egyptian_afterlife_beliefs
Animal magnetism, https://en.wikipedia.org/wiki/Animal_magnetism
Anthroposophy, https://en.wikipedia.org/wiki/Anthroposophy
Augustine, https://en.wikipedia.org/wiki/Augustine_of_Hipp
Avincenna ibn Sina, https://en.wikipedia.org/wiki/Avicenna
Banpo Village, Emily Mark https://www.worldhistory.org/Banpo_Village/
Banpo Village, http://www.chinaculturetour.com/xian/banpo-neolithic-village-banpo-museum.htm
Ben Franklin on Reincarnation, Theosophical Society, https://www.theosociety.org/pasadena/sunrise/46-96-7/cy-ivm.htm
Bridey Murphy, Virginia Tighe, https://en.wikipedia.org/wiki/Bridey_Murphy
Buddha, https://en.wikipedia.org/wiki/The_Buddha
Buddhism, https://en.wikipedia.org/wiki/Buddhism
Buddhism and Karma, Barbara O'Brien, learningreligions.com/Barbara-O-Brien
Buddhism vs Hinduism,

https://www.hinduwebsite.com/buddhism/karma-hinduism-buddhism.asp

Call me by my true names, Tich Nhat Hahn, Thay's Poetry / Please Call Me by My True Names (song & poem) | Plum Village, Plumvillage.org

Cases of the Reincarnation Type with Memories from the Intermission Between Lives, Poonam Sharma and Jim Tucker https://digital.library.unt.edu/ark:/67531/metadc799279/m1/1/

Child's grave is the oldest human burial found in Africa, Jamie Shreve https://www.nationalgeographic.com/science/article/childs-grave-is-the-oldest-human-burial-found-in-africa

Chuang Tzu's Butterfly Story, Charlie Ambler https://thedailyzen.org/2015/06/03/chuang-tzus-butterfly-story/

Clement, https://en.wikipedia.org/wiki/Clement_of_Rome

Comparing Reincarnation Beliefs between Hinduism and Buddhism, Hannah Archer, https://medium.com/@xsm918/comparing-reincarnation-beliefs-between-hinduism-and-buddhism-2cb498c4041a

Creative Choice in Hypnosis, Milton Erickson, archive.org/details/creativechoicein0000eric

Dealings with the Dead, Paschal Randolph https://archive.org/details/dealingswithdead00oran/page/n3/mode/2up

Deep Healing: A Practical Outline of Regression Therapy, Hans TenDam, Deep Healing and Transformation - The International Journal of Regression Therapy (regressionjournal.org)

DNA From 12,000-year-old Skeleton Helps Answer the Question: Who Were the First Americans? Mohi Kumar https://www.smithsonianmag.com/science-nature/dna-12000-year-old-skeleton-helps-answer-question-who-were-first-americans-180951469/

Does Anyone Believe in Reincarnation, Michael Laitman http://laitman.com

Druze, Reincarnation Research https://www.reincarnation-research.com/?s=Druze

Druze, https://en.m.wikipedia.org/wiki/Druze

EARTh Association, https://www.earth-association.org/

Edgar Cayce, https://en.wikipedia.org/wiki/Edgar_Cayce

Egyptian Book of the Dead, Joshua Mark https://www.worldhistory.org/Egyptian_Book_of_the_Dead/

Emile Coue, https://en.wikipedia.org/wiki/%C3%89mile_Cou%C3%A9

ESM Hunter-Gathers and the origins of religion, Hervey C. Peoples, Pavel Duda, and Frank W. Marlowe (source: *researchgate.net*, ESM Hunter-Gatherers and the Origins of Religion (researchgate.net)

Etienne Felx d'Henin de Cuviller, https://en.wikipedia.org/wiki/%C3%89tienne_F%C3%A9lix_d%27Henin_de_Cuvillers

Exploring the secret doctrine of the HP Blavatsky (video) with Pablo Sender – The Philosophical Research Society – YouTube https://www.youtube.com/watch?v=TeuAQkcLoos

Franz Mesmer, https://en.wikipedia.org/wiki/Franz_Mesmer
Greek religious mysteries – Arith Härger – YouTube https://www.youtube.com/watch?v=4WS2mO9LCA0
Haplogroups map, https://en.wikipedia.org/wiki/Haplogroup#/media/File:World_Map_of_Y-DNA_Haplogroups.png
Hazel Denning, Journal of Regression Therapy https://regressionjournal.org/jrt_author/hazel-denning-1920-2008/
Hebrew Bible, https://en.wikipedia.org/wiki/Hebrew_Bible
Henry David Thoreau, https://en.wikipedia.org/wiki/Henry_David_Thoreau
Herodotus, https://en.wikipedia.org/wiki/Herodotus
Hindu karmic beliefs, https://www.hinduwebsite.com/hinduism/h_karma.asp
Hippolyte Bernheim, https://en.wikipedia.org/wiki/Hippolyte_Bernheim
History of hypnosis, https://www.petermabbutt.net/hypnotherapy/history-of-hypnosis/
History of hypnosis, Molly Moon https://www.mollymoonsworld.com/hypnotism/history-of-hypnotism/
History of hypnosis, https://en.wikipedia.org/wiki/History_of_hypnosis
History of magic/Histoire de la magie (1860), Eliphas Levi, Éliphas Lévi - Wikipedia
History of reincarnation: The Ancient and Original Beliefs Revealed, https://reincarnationafterdeath.com/history/
Homo naledi and the Rising Star Cave, Great Valley Museum – YouTube

https://www.youtube.com/watch?v=_lMvLKf98a0
Homo Naledi in Photos: Images of the Small-brained Human Relative, Denise Chow
https://www.livescience.com/59093-homo-naledi-human-relative-photos.html
Hunter-Gatherers and the Origins of Religion, Hervey C. Peoples, Pavel Duda, and Frank W. Marlowe
https://www.ncbi.nlm.nih.gov/pmc/articles/PMC4958132/
Jainism, https://en.wikipedia.org/wiki/Jainism#Scriptures_and_texts
Jainism and types of karma,
https://en.wikipedia.org/wiki/Types_of_Karma_(Jainism)
James Braid,
https://en.wikipedia.org/wiki/James_Braid_(surgeon)
James Esdaile, https://en.wikipedia.org/wiki/James_Esdaile
Jean-Martin Charcot, https://en.wikipedia.org/wiki/Jean-Martin_Charcot
Joseph-Claude-Anthelme Recamier,
https://en.wikipedia.org/wiki/Joseph_R%C3%A9camier
Journal of Regression Therapy,
http://regressionjournal.org/history-of-the-journal
Kabbalah on Judaism and Reincarnation, Yerachmiel Tilles
https://www.chabad.org/kabbalah/article_cdo/aid/380599/Jewish/Judaism-and-Reincarnation.html
Karma in Hinduism,
https://en.wikipedia.org/wiki/Karma_in_Hinduism
Karma in Jainism,
https://en.wikipedia.org/wiki/Karma_in_Jainism
Lionel Giles, https://en.wikipedia.org/wiki/Lionel_Giles

Maxmillian Hell, https://en.wikipedia.org/wiki/Maximilian_Hell

Michael Newton, TNI https://www.newtoninstitute.org/dr-michael-newton/

Michael Teachings, michaelteachings.com

Naia, 12500-year-old skeleton, https://www.sci.news/othersciences/anthropology/science-naia-skeleton-first-americans-01925.html

Names of the Soul, Rabbi Yitzchak Luria https://www.chabad.org/kabbalah/article_cdo/aid/38037/Jewish/Names-of-the-soul_11.html

Neurypnology, James Braid, historyofhypnosis.org/james-braid

Oracle Bones, Emily Mark https://www.worldhistory.org/Oracle_Bones/

Oracle Bones, https://pressbooks.ulib.csuohio.edu/intro-to-chinese-calligraphy/chapter/evolution-of-characters-tools-techniques/

Origen, https://en.wikipedia.org/wiki/Origen

Paracelsus, https://en.wikipedia.org/wiki/Paracelsus

Pierre Janet, https://en.wikipedia.org/wiki/Pierre_Janet

Plato—Understanding His Philosophies and the Allegory of the Cave, Seyone Chithrananda https://seyonec.medium.com/plato-understanding-his-philosophies-and-the-allegory-of-the-cave-501906276b9a

Pythagoras, https://plato.stanford.edu/entries/pythagoras/#Pyt

Pythagorean Views of Existence, James. E. Frey http://www.midnightfreemasons.org/2013/06/pythagorean-views-of-existence.html

Raymond Moody on Reincarnation – Sivananda Ashram Yoga Retreat Bahamas – YouTube https://youtu.be/n_S8yacTRnU
Reincarnation, https://theosophy.wiki/en/Reincarnation#:~:text=in
Reincarnation, www.theosophy.world/encycloopedia/reincarnation
Reincarnation, Rav Berg https://www.kabbalah.com/en/articles/reincarnation
Reincarnation and Afterlife, Rabbi Simon Jacobson www.meaningfullife.com/jewish-reincarnation-beliefs/
Reincarnation and Freemasonry, Bro. Ken JP Stuczynski, The Midnight Freemasons: Reincarnation and Freemasonry
Reincarnation and Karma, HP Blavatsky, Reincarnation and Karma by H.P. Blavatsky (blavatskyarchives.com) www.blavatskyarchives.com/blavatskykarmareincarnation.html
Reincarnation and Native Americans, Caroline Knight https://www.uniguide.com/reincarnation-native-american
Reincarnation in African Traditional Religion, Andrew Rook www.theosophy-nw.org/theosnw/world/afirca/afrook2.htm
Reincarnation in America: A Brief Historical Overview, Lee Irwin https://www.researchgate.net/publication/320339721_Reincarnation_in_America_A_Brief_Historical_Overview
Relief of Amenemhat I from his pyramid complex at El-Lisht, https://en.wikipedia.org/wiki/Amenemhat_I#/media/File:L

intel_of_Amenemhat_I_and_Deities_MET_DP322055.jpg
Researches in Reincarnation and Beyond, A.R. Martin
http://www.christian-reincarnation.com/PDF/Martin.pdf
Retirement and Reincarnation, Dali Lama
https://www.dalailama.com/messages/retirement-and-reincarnation/reincarnation
Ron Jue, Journal of Regression Therapy https://regressionjournal.org/jrt_author/ronald-wong-jue/
Rudolph Steiner,
https://en.wikipedia.org/wiki/Rudolf_Steiner
Shanidar Cave,
https://en.wikipedia.org/wiki/Shanidar_Cave
Shanidar Cave, Varoujan K. Sissakian https://www.researchgate.net/publication/338205868_Shanidar_Cave_-_An_Interesting_Archaeological_Site_in_the_Kurdistan_Region_Iraq
Statue of Senusret I in the Cairo Museum, Egypt, W.M. Flinders Petrie
https://en.wikipedia.org/wiki/Senusret_I#/media/File:Statue_Senusret_I_Petrie.jpg
Taoism and Reincarnation: Why and How Does the Soul Return, https://reincarnationafterdeath.com/taoism/
The Birth of Hypnosis, Ethan Wise
www.wisehypnosis.com/articles/history-of-hypnosis/birth-of-hypnosis
The Phenomenology of 'Solved' Reincarnation Stories Among Druze in
Israel: Private Self, Symbolic Type and Daily Life, Maha Natoor and Avihu Shoshana https://doi.org/10.1007/s11013-021-09711-y

Thelma Freedman, https://regressionjournal.org/jrt_author/thelma-b-freedman/

Valentine Greatrakes, https://en.wikipedia.org/wiki/Valentine_Greatrakes

Vedas: A Brief Introduction, Deepansh Palawat https://theancientpaper.com/vedas-a-breif-introduction/

Waking Hypnosis as a Psychotherapeutic Technique, Warwick D. Phipps https://ngh.net/waking-hypnosis-as-a-psychotherapeutic-technique

Walt Whitman, https://en.wikipedia.org/wiki/Walt_Whitman

William James, https://en.wikipedia.org/wiki/William_James

William Strachey, https://encyclopediavirginia.org/entries/strachey-william-1572-1621/

Winafred Lucas, https://regressionjournal.org/jrt_author/winafred-lucas/

ABOUT THE AUTHOR

Carole Louie is on a spiritual journey. When she overcame her lifelong fear of ghosts to communicate with her father's spirit, her world turned inside out.

An award-winning Interior Designer, Louie juggled the experiences of her spiritual journey with the mundane world. Conversations with her father's ghost helped her accept her gift as a medium. Her explorations into her father's Buddhist beliefs about ghosts and reincarnation inspired her to delve into reincarnation research.

Louie's short story, *I Remember*, was published in the anthology *From Ashes to Healing: Mystical Encounters with the Holocaust*, compiled by Rabbi Yonassan Gershom.

Louie is certified in Past Life Regression Therapy with The Weiss Institute and Carol Bowman and is a Certified Master Hypnotist with HCH Institute. She incorporates her gifts as a medium with her sessions.

The Not-So-Secret Life of Emily Elizabeth, a paranormal mystery, is a cozy fiction based on a composite of past life memories.

Conversations with a Hungry Ghost: Memoir of a Reluctant Medium tells the story of how Louie overcame her lifelong fear of ghosts to speak with her father and how their conversations guided her to his village in Taishan, China.

Her genealogical research continued and led her to the gates of the Forbidden City. She documents her discoveries in *The Legacy of the Lei Family Architects: The Story of Yang-shi Lei.*

Unstuck in Time: Memoir of a Time Traveler is a true story about how love transcends time. It is a spiritual quest through many lives to discover the reasons why we reincarnate and how awareness of other lives can affect the present life.

Louie is the Director of The Center of Reincarnation and Evolution, a center for spiritual growth in Richmond, VA. She offers private sessions, classes, workshops, and events to help others on their spiritual journey. She is the founder of the Reincarnation Symposium, an event that gathers people devoted to research, regression therapy, and who share their stories about remembering or experiences.

For more information, go to carolelouie.net.

END NOTES

[1] Denise Chow. "Homo Naledi in Photos: Images of the Small-Brained Human Relative." *Live Science*, May 12, 2017. https://www.livescience.com/59093-homo-naledi-human-relative-photos.html.

[2] Jamie Shreeve. "Child's Grave is the Oldest Human Burial Found in Africa." *National Geographic*, May 5, 2022. https://www.nationalgeographic.com/science/article/childs-grave-is-the-oldest-human-burial-found-in-africa.

[3] Shreeve, "Child's Grave."

[4] Hervey C. Peoples, Pavel Duda, and Frank W. Marlowe. "Hunter-Gatherers and the Origins of Religion." National Center for Biotechnology Information. Accessed September 14, 2023. https://www.ncbi.nlm.nih.gov/pmc/articles/PMC4958132/.

[5] Harold M. Tanner, *China: A History Vol. 1: From Neolithic through the Great Qing Empire* (Indianapolis: Hackett Publishing Co. Inc., 2010), 40.

[6] Joe Fisher, *The Case for Reincarnation* (Bantam, 1985), 85.

[7] Joseph Head and S. L. Cranston, *Reincarnation: The Phoenix Fire Mystery* (Three Rivers Press, 1976), 113.

[8] James E. Frey, "Pythagorean Views of Existence," Midnight Freemasons, accessed September 30, 2023, http://www.midnight-freemasons.org/2013/06/pythagorean-views-of-existence.html, quoting Eliphas Levi, *History of Magic* (1913).

9 Head and Cranston, *Reincarnation*, 204-205.

10 James Matlock, *Signs of Reincarnation: Exploring Beliefs, Cases, and Theory* (Rowman & Littlefield Publishers, 2019).

11 Chuang Chou, trans. Waley and Giles, in *Reincarnation: The Phoenix Fire Mystery*, Head and Cranston, 111.

12 Head and Cranston, *Reincarnation*, 108.

13 Head and Cranston, *Reincarnation*, 141.

14 Charles Stang, "Flesh and Fire: Reincarnation and Universal Salvation in the Early Church," Harvard Divinity School, March 19, 2019, https://hds.harvard.edu/news/2019/03/19/flesh-and-fire-reincarnation-and-universal-salvation-early-church.

15 Edmond Holmes, *The Albigensian or Catharist Heresy, a Story and a Study* (London: Williams & Norgate, 1925).

16 Rosemary Ellen Guiley, *Encyclopaedia of Mystical and Paranormal Experience* (HarperSanFrancisco, 1991), 501. This was discussed in the "Your Journey was Never Meant to End" Facebook group under a post titled "The Doctrine of Reincarnation of Soul" by Vidya Sagar Verman, former Indian diplomat.

17 Guiley, *Encyclopaedia of Mystical and Paranormal Experience*, 580.

18 Fisher, *Reincarnation*.

19 Antonia Mills and Richard Slobodin, *Amerindian Rebirth: Reincarnation Belief Among North American Indians and Inuit* (University of Toronto Press, 1994).

20 Ken JP Stuczynski, "Reincarnation and Freemasonry," Midnight

The Cosmology of Reincarnation

Freemasons, accessed September 30, 2023, http://www.midnightfreemasons.org/2022/04/reincarnation-and-freemasonry.html.

[21] Benjamin Franklin, "Benjamin Franklin: In His Own Words," Library of Congress, accessed September 30, 2023, https://www.loc.gov/exhibits/franklin/bf-trans61.html.

[22] Ingrid Van Mater, "The Eternal Song of Creation," quoting Benjamin Franklin, Sunrise Magazine, accessed September 30, 2023, https://www.theosociety.org/pasadena/sunrise/46-96-7/cy-ivm.htm.

[23] Lee Irwin, "Reincarnation in America: A Brief Historical Overview," Religions 8, no. 10, 222 (2017): https://www.mdpi.com/2077-1444/8/10/222.

[24] Head and Cranston, *Reincarnation*, 489.

[25] Head and Cranston, *Reincarnation*, 499-529.

[26] Head and Cranston, *Reincarnation*, 66.

[27] Head and Cranston, *Reincarnation*, 67.

[28] Head and Cranston, *Reincarnation*, 373.

[29] Head and Cranston, *Reincarnation*, 374.

[30] Paramahansa Yogananda, "Paramahansa Yogananda Quotes on Reincarnation," yogananda.com.au, accessed September 30, 2023, http://yogananda.com.au/gurus/yoganandaquoteso6b.html.

[31] Fisher, *Reincarnation*.

[32] Thich Nhat Hanh, "Please Call Me by My True Names," Plum Village, accessed October 1, 2023, https://plumvillage.org/articles/please-call-me-by-my-true-names-song-poem.

33 "Jane Roberts," Wikipedia, last modified September 15, 2023, accessed October 1, 2023, https://en.wikipedia.org/wiki/Jane_Roberts.

34 Irwin, "Reincarnation in America."

35 Hannah Archer, "Comparing Reincarnation Beliefs between Hinduism and Buddhism," Medium, March 23, 2018, https://medium.com/@xsm918/comparing-reincarnation-beliefs-between-hinduism-and-buddhism-2cb498c4041a.

36 Dalai Lama, "Reincarnation," Dalai Lama, September 24, 2011, https://www.dalailama.com/messages/retirement-and-reincarnation/reincarnation.

37 "Taoism and Reincarnation: Why and How Does the Soul Return," Reincarnationafterdeath.com, accessed October 1, 2023, http://www.reincarnationafterdeath.com/taoism-reincarnation.

38 Matlock, *Signs of Reincarnation*, 57.

39 Andrew Rooke, "Reincarnation in African Traditional Religion," *Sunrise* magazine, November 1980, reprinted by Theosophical University Press, accessed October 1, 2023, https://www.theosophy-nw.org/theosnw/world/africa/af-rook2.htm.

40 Rooke, "Reincarnation in African Traditional Religion."

41 Matlock, *Signs of Reincarnation*.

42 Rooke, "Reincarnation in African Traditional Religion."

43 Rooke, "Reincarnation in African Traditional Religion."

44 Michael Berg, "A Secret of Reincarnation," *Kabbalah.com*, February 18, 2020, accessed October 1, 2023, https://www.kabbalah.com/en/articles/secret-reincarnation/.

45 Yerachmiel Tilles, "Kabbalah on Judaism and Reincarnation," *Chabad.org*, accessed October 1, 2023, https://www.chabad.org/kabbalah/article_cdo/aid/380599/jewish/Judaism-and-Reincarnation.htm.

46 Rav Berg, "Reincarnation," *Kabbalah.com*, January 4, 2017, accessed October 1, 2023, https://www.kabbalah.com/en/articles/reincarnation/.

47 Berg, "A Secret of Reincarnation."

48 Berg, "Reincarnation."

49 Rabbi Yonassan Gershom, *From Ashes to Healing: Mystical Encounters with the Holocaust* (ARE Press, 1996).

50 "Jewish Reincarnation Beliefs," Meaningful Life Center, accessed October 7, 2023, https://www.meaningfullife.com/jewish-reincarnation-beliefs/

51 Gebhard Fartacek, ed., *Druze Reincarnation Narratives: Previous Life Memories, Discourses, and the Construction of Identities* (Peter Lang, 2021).

52 "Reincarnation and Karma by H. P. Blavatsky (collected from *The Key to Theosophy, The Secret Doctrine*, and H.P.B. Articles)." *Theosophy World*, accessed October 1, 2023, https://www.theosophy.world/resource/reincarnation-and-karma-h-p-blavatsky.

53 "Reincarnation and Karma by H. P. Blavatsky," *Theosophy World*.

54 "Reincarnation and Karma by H. P. Blavatsky," *Theosophy World*.

55 Jane Roberts, *The Nature of Personal Reality: Specific, Practical Techniques for Solving Everyday Problems and Enriching the Life You Know* (New World Library, 1994), 374.

56 Roberts, *The Nature of Personal Reality*, 279.

57 Roberts, *The Nature of Personal Reality*, 285.

58 Roberts, *The Nature of Personal Reality*, 153.

59 Center for Michael Teachings, accessed October 1, 2023, http://www.centerformichaelteachings.org.

60 The Michael Teachings are too complicated to go in-depth here, but for more information, go to themichaelteachings.com and centerformichaelteachings.org.

61 "A History of the Overleaf Chart From the Original Michael Group to the Present: The Legacy of Philip Wittmeyer — Volume 5," *Center for Michael Teachings*, accessed October 1, 2023, http://centerformichaelteachings.org/download/HOLC-Whole.pdf.

62 David Gregg, "Reincarnation: Everything You Need to Know," *The Michael Teachings*, accessed October 1, 2023, https://www.michaelteachings.com/reincarnation.html.

63 Caris Palm Turpen, "The Seven Levels of Karmic Debt," *The Michael Teachings*, accessed October 1, 2023, https://www.michaelteachings.com/7_levels_karmic_debt.html.

64 The Michael Teachings, accessed October 1, 2023, http://www.themichaelteachings.com.

65 Aaron Abke, "Why Do We Reincarnate? (Law of One) // Spiritual Sh*t Podcast," YouTube video, November 18, 2019, https://www.youtube.com/watch?v=4ZUhtN2wu9o (accessed October 5, 2023, at 1:42).

66 Abke, "Why Do We Reincarnate?"

[67] "Glossary," *Law of One*, accessed October 1, 2023, http://www.lawofone.info/glossary.

[68] Toby Wheelock, "Fundamental Ideas from the Law of One Material (90.12)," *Law of One*, accessed October 1, 2023, https://www.lawofone.info/synopsis-prev.php.

[69] Wheelock, "Fundamental Ideas," *Law of One*, https://www.lawofone.info/synopsis-prev.php.

[70] Ian Stevenson, "Unusual Play in Young Children who Claim to Remember Previous Lives," *Journal of Scientific Exploration* 14, no. 4 (2000): 557-570.

[71] Poonam Sharma and Jim Tucker, "Cases of the Reincarnation Type with Memories from the Intermission Between Lives," *Journal of Near-Death Studies* 23, no. 2 (Winter 2004): 101-118.

[72] Joel Whitton and Joe Fisher, *Life Between Life: Scientific Explorations into the Void Separating One Incarnation from the Next* (Dolphin, 1986).

[73] Whitton and Fisher, *Life Between Life*.

[74] David Reeves, "Hypnosis in Ancient Civilizations," Cuyamungue Institute, accessed October 1, 2023, https://www.cuyamungueinstitute.com/articles-and-news/hypnosis-in-ancient-civilizations/.

[75] Serge Kahili King, *Earth Energies: A Quest for the Hidden Power of the Planet* (Quest Books, 1992).

[76] King, *Earth Energies*, 22.

[77] King, *Earth Energies*, 22.

[78] Sarah C.P. Williams, "Study identifies brain areas altered during

hypnotic trances," Stanford Medicine - News Center, July 28, 2016, https://neuroscience.stanford.edu/news/study-identifies-brain-areas-altered-during-hypnotic-trances.

[79] University of Wisconsin-Madison, June 2008, https://news.wisc.edu/newsphotos/davidson08.html.

[80] Williams, "Study identifies brain areas."

[81] Whitton and Fisher, *Life Between Life*.

[82] Moody, Raymond. "Raymond Moody on Reincarnation." YouTube video, 52:28, posted March 6, 2015. https://youtu.be/n_S8yacTRnU.

ANIMA Channel, "Reincarnation according to Pythagoras," YouTube video, 02:53, posted March 4, 2022, https://www.youtube.com/watch?v=ts1GZ4ygUnM.

[83] Fisher, *Reincarnation*.

[84] Matlock, *Signs of Reincarnation*.

[85] Irwin, "Reincarnation in America."

[86] Rich Stammler, "History of the International Journal of Regression Therapy (JRT)," November 2014, http://regressionjournal.org/history-of-the-journal/.

[87] "Deep Memory Process DMP®," Roger Woolger, accessed October 2, 2023, https://rogerwoolger.org/.

[88] Whitton and Fisher, *Life Between Life*, 6.

[89] Carol Bowman, "Past Life Exploration and Discovery," accessed October 2, 2023, https://www.carolbowman.com/.

[90] The Earth Association for Regression Therapy, accessed October 2, 2023, https://www.earth-association.org/.

[91] Eric J. Christopher, "Exploring the Effectiveness of Past-Life Therapy," 2000

[92] Eric J. Christopher, "Exploring the Effectiveness of Past-Life Therapy," 2000, 14-16

[93] Eric J. Christopher, "Exploring the Effectiveness of Past-Life Therapy," 2000, 31-32

[94] Eric J. Christopher, "Exploring the Effectiveness of Past-Life Therapy," 2000, 19

[95] Eric J. Christopher, "Exploring the Effectiveness of Past-Life Therapy," 2000, 23

[96] Eric J. Christopher, "Exploring the Effectiveness of Past-Life Therapy," 2000, 33-34

[97] Eric J. Christopher, "Exploring the Effectiveness of Past-Life Therapy," 2000, 35

Made in the USA
Las Vegas, NV
30 May 2024

90500922R00095